WRITING STRATEGIES
Reaching Diverse Audiences

LAUREL RICHARDSON
The Ohio State University

Qualitative Research Methods
Volume 21

SAGE PUBLICATIONS
The International Professional Publishers
Newbury Park   London   New Delhi

To Betty Frankle Kirschner

For information address:

SAGE Publications, Inc.
2111 West Hillcrest Drive
Newbury Park, California 91320

SAGE Publications Ltd.
28 Banner Street
London EC1Y 8QE
England

SAGE Publications India Pvt. Ltd.
M-32 Market
Greater Kailash I
New Delhi 110 048 India

Printed in the United States of America

Library of Congress Cataloging-in-Publication Data

Richardson, Laurel.
    Writing strategies : reaching diverse audiences / Laurel
Richardson.
        p.   cm. -- (Qualitative research methods ; 21)
    Includes bibliographical references and index.
    ISBN 0-8039-3521-8 (c). -- ISBN 0-8039-3522-6 (p)
    1. Authorship.   I. Title.   II. Series: Qualitative research
methods ; v. 21.
PN145.R47   1990
808'.02--dc20   90-8771
                                                                    CIP

FIRST PRINTING, 1990

Sage Production Editor: Susan McElroy

CONTENTS

EDITORS' INTRODUCTION

It is well known that all social relations are complexly mediated by symbols. Among the most important of these symbols are written words. We are beginning to learn more about this process of symbolization. Until recently, the interpretation of literature, matters of form and content, had been left to literary critics and essayists. In the late 1970s, however, under the influence of Roland Barthes, this situation changed, and the sociology of literature became a field in the larger enterprise of textual interpretation. Changes were taking place also in the social sciences, where attention was turned to matters of writing itself — the style, the perspective, the metaphors and tropes employed by social science authors. Some of the once clear lines drawn between science, poetry, and fiction were blurred by a growing recognition that all forms of writing contain selective, metaphoric, and expressive aspects as well as being a craft sustained by self-conscious writers. This means that fieldwork and writing on the basis of fieldwork shape and are shaped by stylistic conventions — ways of writing.

Laurel Richardson powerfully advances our understanding of the craft of writing in this 21st volume of the Sage Qualitative Research Methods Series. In *Writing Strategies: Reaching Diverse Audiences* Richardson joins others in the series such as Norman Denzin (volume 17) and Peter Manning (volume 7), who also are concerned with how symbols and their organization convey meaning and a context for social action. Unlike the other monographs, however, this is a very personal, reflexive, and purposive book that carefully considers writing as a craft. Especially illuminating is Richardson's discussion of how to develop and maintain a style of writing when one is working over field or interview notes in an effort to construct an article or book. Rich examples are provided to show how to develop an argument from field materials, how to craft a text for different audiences, and how to polish a draft to produce a persuasive work.

In sum, Laurel Richardson has created a monograph that describes how writing of various kinds is accomplished. By drawing on her own research and writing experience, she self-consciously explicates the fragile line from data to concept to text and back. This is one of the most problematic aspects of social research and one that many young scholars (and seasoned ones as well) have difficulty mastering. It is a good place to begin and to end.

— Peter K. Manning
John Van Maanen
Marc L. Miller

PREFACE AND ACKNOWLEDGMENTS

I wrote this book because I needed to read it. After writing up an intensive interview project for diverse audiences, I was drained and querulous, unsure about *what* I wanted to write next, *how* I wanted to write it, and *who* I wanted to write it for. I turned, at first with curiosity and then with passion, to contemporary theory in philosophy, rhetoric, communication, anthropology, sociology, and literature, and, then, to practical guides for writing. *Writing Strategies: Reaching Diverse Audiences* is the result.

Writing Strategies is intended for both experienced and novice researchers and can be used in graduate methods or theory classes, as well as in practice- and policy-oriented classes. The book is divided into two parts: Theoretical Issues and Practical Solutions. In Theoretical Issues, I discuss contemporary writing issues; the historical separation of science and literature as different writing genres; the new rhetoric; literary devices used in science and social science writing; the use of narrative within social science writing; and authority and authorship. In the second part, Practical Solutions, I shift gears and address, ex post facto, the writing decisions I made in my own work. I present concrete examples of how literary devices work in trade books, academic articles, and articles for mass circulation. The theoretical issues are, thus, linked to practical, writerly problems.

I have loved writing this book — reading for it, thinking about writerly problems, talking to friends, colleagues, and students. There are many people to thank, some of whom may not realize how helpful they have been in providing a nudge, a reference, a supportive or critical comment. These include David Altheide, Maria T. Ammoni, Norman Brown, Suzanne Damarin, Carolyn Ellis, David Maines, Norman Denzin, William Form, John Johnson, Marilyn Johnston, Mary Leach, Patricia Lynch, Peter Manning, Katherine Meyer, Kathleen Nucio, Linda Raphael, Roberta Sands, Dianne Small, John Stewart, Verta Taylor, Carol Warren, and Amy Zaharlick. Graduate students in theory and methods courses over the past few years are especially appreciated. And special thanks go to my generous and able colleagues Eloise A. Buker, Gisela J. Hinkle, and Patti Lather.

Very special thanks go to four people. Betty Frankle Kirschner, to whom this book is dedicated, has been a seriously good friend and unflinching supporter of my writing projects over the past two decades. Writing matters to her, deeply. Mitch Allen has been an exemplary editor — present but not obtrusive. John Van Maanen, the Qualitative Research Methods Series Editor, has shown great forbearance, not to mention great insight and practical

7

guidance. He is one good reader. Finally, Ernest Lockridge has patiently lived with a woman on the edge of postmodernism, read and reread her manuscripts, critiqued them with great care and intelligence, and brought her food and comfort during the worst of the writing sieges. My deepest thanks.

INTRODUCTION

The question is not whether we will write the lives of people — as social scientists that is what we do — but *how* and for *whom*. We choose how we write, and the choices we make do make a difference to ourselves, to social science, and to the people we write about.

Writing matters — theoretically and practically. The goal of this monograph is to link contemporary theoretical issues about writing with practical strategies *for* writing for different audiences — professional, trade, and mass circulation. It does so in two ways: First, this monograph uncovers the writing practices of social science, foregrounding the narrative, literary, and value-constituting structures within it; and, second, it illustrates, with concrete examples, how writing choices work within different texts to reach different audiences.

How *should* we write our research? *Who* is our audience? The rhetorical, ethical, and methodological issues implicit in that question are neither few nor trivial. Rather, the question reflects a central contemporary realization: all knowledge is socially constructed. Writing is not simply a true representation of an objective reality, out there, waiting to be seen. Instead, through literary and rhetorical structures, writing creates a particular view of reality. By what criteria should we evaluate the text? It's scientific soundness? Aesthetic resonance? Ethical rightness? What are our goals? How do we achieve them?

Life histories, informants' oral accounts, in-depth interviews, case studies, historical documents, surveys, and participant observation are the major methods used by social researchers. An abundant literature discusses how to gain entry, write questions, ask questions, listen, take field notes, and tape-record. The tapes and notes, however, do not constitute the "findings." Rather, as part of our *research* agenda, we fashion these materials into a prose piece; we transform biographical interviews, historical documents, census data, and field notes into a sociological text. Although this stage of the research process requires complex decision making, there is little research direction about writing issues and their resolutions (but see Agger, 1990; Becker, 1986; Fox, 1985; Long, 1988; Stewart, 1989; Van Maanen, 1988). Most of the writing about writing, however, has looked at either practical tips or writing theory — not at the interplay between the two. The intention of this monograph is to help fill this methodological gap by linking theoretical writing issues and practical writing strategies.

I will argue that social scientific writing depends upon narrative structure and narrative devices, although that structure and those devices are frequently masked by a scientific frame, which is itself a metanarrative (see Lyotard, 1979). Although a life is not a narrative, people make sense of their lives and the lives of others through narrative constructions. In our work as researchers we weigh and sift experiences, make choices regarding what is significant, what is trivial, what to include, what to exclude. We do not simply chronicle "what happened next," but place the "next" in a meaningful context. By doing so, we craft narratives; we write lives.

At issue, then, is not whether social sciences should use the narrative but what narratives will be provided to the reader, and what readers will we write for. We have many exemplars: the sweeping historical and human drama told by a sociological master, such as Kai Erikson in *Everything in Its Path* (1976); narratives that engage the reader in the daily lives of others, such as the ethnographic classics *Street Corner Society* (Whyte, 1943), *Tally's Corner* (Liebow, 1967), *All Our Kin* (Stack, 1974), *Men and Women of the Corporation* (Kanter, 1980), and *The Mirror Dance* (Krieger, 1983); narratives that engage the reader in subjective worlds through interview materials and accounts such as in *Worlds of Pain* (Rubin, 1976), *The Children of Sanchez* (Lewis, 1970), and *The Ageless Self* (Kaufman, 1986); the shaded narratives of abstract, atemporal, unseen "social forces" that conventional logico-empirical social science tells; and the breezy, pithy stories found in the mass magazines. What strategies can we use to write lives so that our writing matters?

Part I of this monograph, Theoretical Issues, introduces some contemporary writing issues; discusses the historical separation of science and literary writing; analyzes the literary devices used in science and social science writing, including metaphor and synecdoche; describes narrative and provide examples of five different kinds of social scientific narrative; and evaluates the issues around "authority" and "authorship." In Part II, Practical Solutions, the tone changes somewhat, as I reflect upon my own writing strategies and provide concrete examples for shaping the same qualitative research material into different texts for different audiences, academic and lay. I use my own texts as examples because of my familiarity with them. I hasten to say that much of that analysis I construct now — after the fact, self-reflexively, after pondering the theoretical issues that frame the practical resolutions.

WRITING STRATEGIES
Reaching Diverse Audiences

LAUREL RICHARDSON
The Ohio State University

PART I

Theoretical Issues

1. CONTEMPORARY WRITING ISSUES

As social scientists, we work within, not above, broader historical, social, and intellectual contexts. These contexts serve as frames for the questions we ask, and the answers we get. Characteristic of the current context is the loss of authority and the loss of "a general paradigmatic style for organizing research" (see Marcus and Fisher, 1986, p. 8). This context has been given the somewhat oxymoronic label of "postmodernism" (see Haraway, 1988; Hassan, 1987; Richardson, 1990).

The postmodernist stance challenges claims to a singular, correct style for doing and presenting research and rejects the Enlightenment's faith in progress through education and rationality. All academic disciplines, to various degrees, have been affected by the postmodernist critique of what constitutes knowledge (truth, beauty, the "canon"), and how and for whom knowledge is created. (See for literary criticism, Eagleton, 1983; Morris, 1988; for the arts, Lather, 1988; for philosophy, Rorty, 1979; for physics, Gleick, 1984; for mathematics, Kline, 1980; for social sciences, Agger, 1989a; Buker, in press; Clifford and Marcus, 1986; Denzin, 1986; Harding, 1986; Hutcheon, 1988; McCloskey, 1985; Nicholson, 1990; Rogers, 1989).

When the foundations of knowledge are themselves open to contextualization and indeterminacy, researchers have a "crisis of representation," uncertainty about what constitutes adequate depiction of social reality (Marcus and Fisher, 1986, p. 8). For social scientists, the problem is not simply devising better techniques and instruments for apprehending social reality, since writing up what one has apprehended is itself a central theoretical and methodological problematic. How do we write (explain, describe, index) the social? (see Brown, 1977; Edmondson, 1984; Richardson, in press-b; Van Maanen, 1988). Language is not simply "transparent," reflecting a social reality that is objectively out there. Rather, language is a *constitutive* force, creating a particular view of reality. All language has grammatical, narrative, and rhetorical structures that construct the subjects and objects of our research, bestow meaning, and create value. This is as true for writing as it is for speaking, and as true of science as it is of poetry.

Producing "things" always involves values — what things to produce, what to regard as equivalents, who has the right to name the things, and who defines the relationship between the "things" and the people who name them (see Shapiro, 1985-1986). Writing "things" is no exception. Writing always involves what Roland Barthes refers to as "the ownership of the means of enunciation" (quoted in Shapiro, 1985-1986, p. 195). A disclosure of writing practices, thus, is always a disclosure of forms of power (Derrida, 1982). Power is, always, a sociohistorical construction. No textual staging is ever innocent. We are always inscribing values in our writing. It is unavoidable.

When we write social science, we are using our authority and privileges to tell about the people we study (Richardson, in press-b). No matter how we stage the text, we — as authors — are doing the staging. As we speak about the people we study, we also speak for them. As we inscribe their lives, we bestow meaning and promulgate values. I shall return to this authority issue later. But, now, let us turn to specific science writing issues.

2. SCIENCE WRITING

When we write science, whether we recognize it or not, we write a narrative and create some kind of narrative meaning. Narrative, as understood here, is not confined to literature or case studies but is one of the two basic and universal cognitive modes — the other being the logico-scientific (Bruner, 1986). "Narrative meaning is created by noting that something is a part of the whole and that something is a cause of something else" (Polkinghorne, 1988, p. 6). Unlike the logico-scientific mode, which looks for universal truth conditions, the narrative mode is contextually embedded and looks for particular connections between events. The *connections* between the *events* is the *meaning*.

Whenever we write science, we are telling some kind of story, or some part of a larger narrative. Some of our stories are more complex, more densely described, and offer greater opportunities as emancipatory documents; others are more abstract, distanced from lived experience, and reinscribe existent hegemonies. Even when we think we are not telling a story, we are, at the very least, embedding our research in a metanarrative, about, for example, how science progresses or how art is accomplished (Lyotard, 1979). Even the shape of the conventional research report reveals a narratively driven subtext: theory (literature review) is the past or the (researcher's) cause for the present study (the hypothesis being tested), which will lead to the future — findings and implications (for the researcher, the researched, and science). Narrative structures, therefore, are preoperative regardless of whether one is writing primarily in the narrative or logico-scientific mode.

Scientists often resist recognizing that their writings are particular kinds of narratives and that their writing practices are value constituting. Rather, they can easily be "duped" by their own writing practices, which suppresses how real people (the researchers) are ordering and constituting reality, because they draw upon the *logico*-scientific code (Bruner, 1986), which represents itself as objective and true. But we should not be fooled. Science writing, like all other forms of writing, is a sociohistorical construction that is narratively driven and depends upon literary devices not just for adornment but for *cognitive* meaning.

Let me, now, briefly narrate the history of the separation of science and literature, before attending to the rhetorical and literary devices within science writing and a much fuller explication of narrative within social science.

Scientific Writing in Historical Context

Since the seventeenth century, the world of writing has been divided into two separate kinds: literary and scientific. From the seventeenth century onward, literature was associated with fiction, rhetoric, and subjectivity, whereas science was associated with fact, "plain language," and objectivity (Clifford, 1986, p. 5). Fiction was "false" because it invented reality, unlike science, which was "true," because it simply reported reality, that which scientists observed. Because literature depended upon the evocative devices of metaphor, different readers could interpret the writing in different ways. The desired unambiguous voice of science was violated by literature where a writer willfully said "one thing to illuminate something else" (De Certau, 1983, p. 178).

Abetted by Plato's expulsion of poets in his *Republic,* assaults upon literary writing intensified during the eighteenth century. John Locke cautioned adults to forego figurative language lest the "conduit" between "things" and "thought" be obstructed. He urged parents to stifle poetic tendencies in their children. Science, in Locke's estimation, was of greater value and had to be written in plain style, in words that did not "move the Passions and thereby mislead the Judgement," unambiguous words unlike the "perfect cheats" of poetic utterances (quoted in Levine, 1985, p. 3). David Hume depicted poets as professional liars. Jeremy Bentham proposed that the ideal language would be one without words, only unambiguous symbols. Samuel Johnson's dictionary sought to fix "univocal meanings in perpetuity, much like the univocal meanings of standard arithmetic terms" (Levine, 1985, p. 4). This is the linguistic world into which the Marquis de Condorcet introduced the term "social science." De Condorcet contended that with precision in language about moral and social issues "knowledge of the truth" would be "easy and error almost impossible" (quoted in Levine, 1985, p. 6). Both positivist and interpretive sociologists agreed. Emile Durkheim wanted sociology to cleanse itself of everyday language. Max Weber urged the construction of ideal types as a way to achieve the univocality of science. The search for the unambiguous was "the triumph of the quest for certainty over the quest for wisdom" (Rorty, 1979, p. 61).

By the nineteenth century, literature and science stood as two separate domains. Literature was aligned with art and culture. It contained the values of "taste, aesthetics, ethics, humanity, and morality" (Clifford, 1986, p. 6) and the rights to metaphoric and ambiguous language. Given to science was the belief that its words were objective, precise, unambiguous, non-contextual, nonmetaphoric. This is the Faustian bargain that has birthed modern "core" sociology and its homunculus, "midwestern empiricism" (Agger, 1989b).

The Rhetoric of Science

The historical separation of literature and science, however, is not immutable. Today, scholars in a host of disciplines are doing major deconstructive and reconstructive analyses of scientific and literary writing. Their analyses concretely show where and how literary devices are used in science writing. I present this material to lessen the grasp that the idea of "objective" writing has on both quantitative and qualitative writers.

Some of the most powerful analyses are coming from the new rhetoric, also known as the rhetoric of inquiry (see Nelson, Megill, and McCloskey, 1987). The new rhetoric makes two assumptions: first that all writing shares common rhetorical devices such as metaphor, imagery, invocations to authority, and appeals to audience; and second, that each field has its own set of literary devices and rhetorical appeals such as theorems, invisible hands, probability tables, archival records, and first-hand experience, which are themselves rhetorically constructed. Rhetorical devices are not ornamental but instrumental in the "persuasive discourse" of science. Any time words are used, technical writing problems are involved, including the use of rhetoric. "The only road from grammar to logic . . . runs through the intermediate territory of rhetoric" (Frye, 1957, p. 331). Science does not stand in opposition to rhetoric; it uses it. And, conversely, the use of rhetoric is not irrational.

Resistance to the idea of rhetoric in science, however, is strong and is related to the modernist belief in the transparency of language. Intellectual inheritors of the seventeenth century insist that language is intrinsically irrelevant to the scientific enterprise. Like a clear pane of glass, science writing presumably neither distorts nor smudges reality but aims to let "the audience see the external world as it is" (Gusfield, 1976, p. 17). Reality is conceived of as standing outside and independent of any observation of or writing about it. The conduit between thing and thought is unobstructed. This modernist belief in the externality of facts and the neutrality of language, however, is out of step with contemporary *scientific* thought about science and its construction. Werner Heisenberg, the author of the "uncertainty principle," for example, states, "Science no longer confronts nature as an objective observer, but sees itself as an actor in this interplay between man and nature" (Heisenberg, 1965, p. 446).

Modernist visions of science writing are also blind to the actual practices of science—rhetorical practices that exist in all the sciences, but vary throughout the centuries (see Nelson et al., 1987). A particularly valuable example of the rhetorical construction of science is Charles Darwin's *On The Origin of Species*. Darwin was well aware, as his writer's notebooks tell us, of the importance of rhetorical staging in constituting scientific ideas. The notebooks reveal Darwin the scientist-rhetorician. Darwin consciously wrote *Origins* according to the scientific conventions of his time, "Baconian induction and quasi-positivistic standards of proof" (Campbell, 1987, pp. 72-73). He purposefully insisted "that his ideas were the results of 'facts' and his metaphors mere expressions of convenience" (Campbell, 1987, p. 72). Darwin's insistence that he was simply a naturalist gathering facts and working inductively, however, is belied by his notebooks. He had a theory and wanted to solve a theoretical problem — not marshal facts. Disclaimers that his metaphoric language was merely "convenient," moreover, are contravened by his own nonpositivisitic theories of language. He suppressed how he did his work and why he wrote as he did, because he knew these aberrations would impugn his credibility. He chose to report his work within the methodological conventions important to his colleagues. The protective coloration of scientific conventions disguised Darwin's heretical ideas and contributed to the survival of his thesis.

Styles of writing science are not fixed or neutral but reflect the historically shifting domination of particular schools or paradigms. Darwin's style, today, would doom his writing to extinction because the sciences have adopted different rhetorical conventions. This is quite evident in the American Psychological Association's *Publication Manual,* 200 pages of rules ranging from punctuation to content and organization. The currently prescribed style gained ascendancy simultaneously with the ascendancy of behaviorist psychology. The articles have become increasingly narrow in scope and focused on a little bit of knowledge — as though knowledge "really" were a bin of bits. The main unifying theme is the hypothesis, which might be repeated up to four times. The repetition elicits a response. The official style institutionalizes behavioristic assumptions about writers, readers, subjects, and knowledge itself. "The prescribed style grants all the participants exactly the role they have in a behavioristic universe" (Bazerman, 1988, p. 126).

All the social sciences have prescribed writing formats — none of them neutral, all of them value constituting. *How* we are expected to write affects *what* we can write about. The referencing system in the social sciences discourages the use of footnotes, a place for secondary arguments, novel conjectures, and related ideas. Incorporated into the text, albeit in parentheses, are the publication dates for citations, as though this information counts the most. Knowledge is constituted as focused, problem (i.e., hypothesis) centered, linear, straightforward. Other thoughts are extraneous. Inductively accomplished research is to be reported deductively; the argument is to be abstractable in 150 words or less; and researchers are to identify explicitly with a theoretical-methodological label. Each of these conventions favors — creates and sustains — a particular vision of what constitutes sociological knowledge. The conventions hold tremendous material and symbolic power over social scientists. Using them increases the probability of one's work being accepted into core social science journals, but they are not prima facie evidence of greater — or lesser — truth value or significance than social science writing using other conventions.

3. LITERARY DEVICES IN SOCIAL SCIENCE WRITING

Social science writing, like all writing, depends upon literary and rhetorical devices to articulate its ideas and make its point, convincingly, credibly, and cognitively. Social science does this, as does all writing, partially by prefiguring its ideas through literary or rhetorical tropes. Two of the most important tropes are synecdoche and metaphor. Neither is merely ornamental. Both tropes convey the credibility of the work and its *cognitive* content. If we believe we know something, then tropes are at work.

Synecdoche

Synecdoche is a rhetorical technique through which a part comes to stand for the whole, such as an individual for a class. Examples are "roof" standing for "house," the "gavel" for the "law," "graybeard" for a "wise old man," and so on. Synecdoches are ways in which we construct our understanding of the whole, although we only have access to the part. Synecdoches are part of our general cultural heritage and exist in literature as well as science. Archetypes, mythic characters, gods and goddesses have all been viewed as synecdochical, as have some literary characters, such as Hamlet, Lady Macbeth, Othello, Desdemona, Romeo, Juliet, Jane Eyre, and Willy Loman.

Within science writing, synecdoches are common as well. For example, DNA is a synecdoche for life, the test tube for experiment, the statistical test for proof, and Tally's corner for a kind of social organization. Social science reasoning, generally — indeed science reasoning — is based on synecdoche, because we are usually studying parts, examples, experiments, or samples, which we intend to represent a whole. Because this is the typical method of reasoning within social science, its existence and power as a literary device within science goes almost unnoticed. I shall return to this again, later.

Metaphor

Metaphor is the backbone of social science writing, and like a true spine, it bears weight, permits movement, links parts together into a functional, coherent whole — and is not immediately visible. Without metaphor, writing is spineless. But, due to the strength of the logico-empiricist beliefs about writing, we often do not recognize metaphor's role in social science analysis.

"The essence of metaphor is understanding and experiencing one kind of thing in terms of another" (Lakoff and Johnson, 1980, p. 5). This is accomplished through comparison or analogy, e.g., "my love is like a red, red rose," or "the evening of life." More subtly and more relevant to conventional social science writing, the metaphor can be carried implicitly in everyday plain language. Consider the following statements about theory (examples based on Lakoff and Johnson, 1980, p. 46): "What is the *foundation* of your theory?" "Your theory needs more *support.*" "Your position is *shaky.*" "Your argument is *falling apart.*" "Let's *construct* an argument." "The *form* of the argument needs *buttressing.*" "Given your *framework,* no wonder your argument *fell apart.*"

The italicized words in the preceding paragraph are expressions that convey the metaphor "theory is a building." This customary way of talking about theory presupposes a metaphor that we are usually unconscious of using. Moreover, the metaphor structures the actions we take in theorizing and what we believe constitutes theory. We try to *build* a theoretical *structure,* which we then experience as a *structure,* which has a *form* and *foundation,* which we then experience as an *edifice,* sometimes quite *grand,* sometimes in need of *shoring up,* and sometimes in need of *dismantling* or, more recently, *deconstructing.* Consider how differently we would experience theory, if the metaphor were "theory is a feather." Or, who might be considered capable of theorizing if theory were metaphored as "like life."

The *truth value* of science writing, moreover, partially depends upon a deep epistemic code regarding "the way that knowledge and understanding *in general* are figured" (Shapiro, 1985-1986, p. 198). Metaphors and figures of speech external to the particular piece of research prefigure the analysis with a code belonging to another domain (Jameson, 1981). For example, the use of "enlighten" or "idea" for knowledge is a light-based metaphor, what Derrida (1982) refers to as the heliocentric view of knowledge, the passive receipt of rays. Imminent in these tropes, Derrida argues, are philosophical and value commitments so entrenched and familiar that they can do their partisan work in the guise of neutrality, passing as literal.

Metaphors exist at the conceptual level and prefigure judgments about the truth value of a social science text. Positivist-empiricism, the "guiding light" of the social sciences, uses three metaphors, which remove the datum from the temporal and human practices that produced it (Shapiro, 1985-1986). First is the grammatical split between subject and object, a wholly unnoticed metaphor for the separation between "real" subjects and objects. The metaphor is particularly powerful because it is a part of our language structure. It "fixes" things in time and space. Second, empiricism views language as a *tool*. The empiricist world is fixed and available for viewing through the instrumentality of language, downplaying that *what* we speak about is partly a function of *how* we speak. Third, empiricism uses a *management* metaphor. Data are managed, variables are manipulated, research is designed, time is flow-charted, tables are produced, and models (like toothpaste and cars) are tested. The three metaphors work together to reify a radical separation between subject and object and to create a static world of "things," fixed in time and space. In this world, the "knower" is estranged from the "known"; intellectual inquiry becomes a matter of precise observation and measurement of what is objectively out there. Not surprisingly, these metaphors coalesce with empiricism's transparency metaphor regarding language.

Metaphor does not stop at the philosophical level but enters each stage of social scientific reasoning. Social scientists construct a social world that is thought to be like a complex model whose measurements are like the proxy variables at hand. "The complex model is said to be like a simpler model for actual thinking, which is in turn like an even simpler model for calculation" (McCloskey, 1985, p. 75). The analogic structure is aided by the use of other rhetorical devices such as the ordering of material, the use of examples to prove the general case, the construction of ideal or test cases, repetition (e.g., of the hypothesis), appeals to authorities (citations), and so on (see Edmondson, 1984).

Metaphors are everywhere. "Functionalism," "role" theory, "game" theory, "dramaturgical analogy," "organicism," "social evolutionism," the social "system," social "structure," "ecology," "labeling" theory are obviously metaphoric. Conceptually, we talk about "equilibrium," "human capital," the "power elite," "resource mobilization," ethnic "insurgency," "developing" countries, "stratification," and so on. Methodologically, we talk about the "power" of a test and statistical "significance" (as distinct from sociological significance); we "sample" a "target" population that we "survey" and "probe." Metaphors organize social scientific work and affect the interpretations of the facts; indeed, facts are interpretable (make sense) only in terms of their place within a metaphoric structure. The sense making is always value constituting — making sense in a particular way, privileging one ordering of the facts over others.

As social science is written in its "flagship" journals, metaphors work together to create an image of a particular kind of sociology as the presumptively standard and correct sociology. A *systematic* approach is consistent with the metaphor of a *social system.* There are *variables* and *indicators* that can be *treated* and *manipulated. Paradigms* (like managers?) are judged by their *power* at *handling* problems. And like managers, paradigms decide which problems are "real" and "important" ones. In the ecological-demographic world, which has increasing currency in sociology, the family is defined as a *cluster* of persons in relationship to a *marker;* populations are a *set* of individuals in an *interdependent system* of *functions. Production* of *outputs* is based on *ingredients* called *inputs.* Human beings are metaphored out of this world. Metaphored in are some rather reassuring (and self-serving) values — such as, the *social* world is controllable, and sociologists can *control* it.

What social science has tried unsuccessfully to keep out of its writing may very well be the proper approach to and subject matter of the discipline. No matter how plain-spoken social scientists try to be, the unavoidable human content keeps invading their thinking and shaping their writing. The marker, the handler, the controller, the human body is present in the sentences social scientists write and appears every time they break out in prose. Narrative is unavoidable.

4. NARRATIVE

Narrative displays the goals and intentions of human actors; makes individuals, cultures, societies, and historical epochs comprehensible as wholes; humanizes time; allows us to contemplate the effects of our actions and to alter the directions of our lives. Narrative is everywhere, present in myth, fable, short story, epic, history, tragedy, comedy, painting, dance, stained glass windows, cinema, social histories, fairy tales, novels, science schema, comic strips, conversation, journal articles. Children everywhere learn how to listen to and tell stories at very early ages. Roland Barthes comments, "The narratives of the world are without number. . . . The narrative is present at all times, in all places, in all societies: the history of narrative begins with the history of [hu]mankind; there does not exist, and never has existed, a people without narratives" (Barthes, 1966, p. 14).

Narrative is the primary way through which humans organize their experiences into temporally meaningful episodes (Polkinghorne, 1988, p. 1). People link events narratively. The meaning of each event is produced by its temporal position and role in a comprehensible whole. Narratively, to answer the question, "What does something *mean*?" requires showing how the something contributed to the conclusion of the episode. The connections between the events is the meaning.

Narrative is both a mode of reasoning and a mode of representation. People can apprehend the world narratively and people can tell about the world narratively. Narrative, as discussed earlier, is one of two basic and universal human cognition modes—the other being the logico-scientific. The two modes are irreducible to each other, and complementary. Each mode provides a distinctive way of ordering experience and constructing reality; each has its own operating principles and criteria of "well-formedness"; and each has radically different procedures for verification (Bruner, 1986). Causality plays a central role in both cognitive modes, but they define it differently. Unlike the logico-scientific mode, which looks for universal truth conditions, the narrative mode is contextually embedded and looks for particular connections between events. The narrative code demonstrates narrative reasoning, the type of reasoning that understands the whole by the integration of its parts, whereas the logico-scientific code demonstrates empiricist reasoning, the type of reasoning that proves statements (Jakobson, 1960). Both modes, however, are framed in metanarratives such as science, the enlightenment, or religion. Narrative structures, therefore, frame both narrative and logico-scientific writings.

Given the unavoidability of narrative within the social sciences, and given how human values, sensibilities, and ambiguities continuously reassert themselves in plain writing, we are propelled into taking seriously the relevance of narrative to the sociological enterprise. Narrative cannot be suppressed within the human sciences because it is ineluctably tied to the human experience; trying to suppress it undermines the very foundation of the human sciences.

Everywhere people experience and interpret their lives in relationship to *time*. Time is the quintessential basis for and constraint upon the human experience. And everywhere humans make sense of their temporal worlds through the narrative. The philosopher Paul Ricoeur (1984-1986) has noted the relationship between the human experience of time and the universality of the narrative. Ricoeur's thesis is that the coexistence of the temporal nature of the human being and the activity of narrating a story are not accidental but represent a "transcultural form of necessity" (p. 52). Through the narrative, temporality becomes interpretable in human terms. Time is made human; narrative is a condition of temporal experience.

Unlike the clock and calendars that measure out life in moments, days, and years, people do not experience time as a succession of instants, a linear linking of points in space, but as extended awareness of the past and the future within the present (see Husserl, 1964). Sometimes time is experienced as a concordant whole, such as when reading a familiar poem, where the whole piece is experienced despite the fact that some of it has already been read and more is yet to come. Other times time is experienced as discordant, such as when regret about the past or fear of the future impinge upon the present. This discordance cannot ever be totally overcome because human knowledge includes the knowledge that one's days are numbered. The future always becomes the past. The future is always death.

Narrative provides powerful access to this uniquely human experience of time in five sociologically significant ways: the everyday; the autobiographical; the biographical; the cultural; and what I term the collective story. Although I present these ways as analytically separable, in practice they can overlap and intersect, as for example when interviewees tell their autobiography, which the interviewer writes up as a biography but presents as part of a more general cultural or collective story.

Everyday Life

In everyday life, narrative articulates how actors go about their rounds and accomplish their tasks. The narrative of "what we did today" assumes an experience of time. We had time to, we took time for, we lost time. We organize our days with temporal markers, such as first, then, and after. Our experience of daily time links us to others and to the public world. We meet people at particular times, we get caught in rush-hour traffic, we watch the six o'clock news. Social order is sustained through these collaborative efforts of individuals timing the logistics of their daily activities. People routinely talk to each other by accounting for how they spent their day — (What did you do in school today? What happened at work today?). Ethnomethodologists and conversational analysts have been especially attuned to these quotidian accounts, and a large research literature exists based on those perspectives. Few of these researchers, however, have explicitly analyzed and articulated how the individual's narrated experiences of daily time are linked to larger social structures, the personal to the public.

Autobiography

Second, autobiographically, narrative is how people articulate how the past is related to the present. Events have a beginning, a middle, and an end. The past can be retrieved and relived in the present. Narrative organizes that experience of time into personal historicity. "Autobiography is the highest and most instructive form in which the understanding of life is confronting us" (Dilthey, quoted in Kohli, 1981, p. 63). Telling one's story gives meaning to the past from the point of view of the present and future, and "deeply gives meaning to the past in order to give meaning to the present life of the person" (Bertaux-Wiame, 1981).

People organize their personal biographies and understand them through the stories they create to explain and justify their life experiences. When people are asked why they do what they do, they provide narrative explanations, not logico-scientific categorical ones. It is the way individuals understand their own lives and best understand the lives of others. Experiences are connected to other experiences and evaluated in relation to the larger whole. Something does not make sense when it does not fit in with the narrative. To make sense of the events in their lives, people reconstruct biography. The experience of renarrativizing — like the experience of biographical time itself — is open ended and polysemous, where different meanings and systems of meanings can emerge.

Narrative functions at the autobiographical level to mark off one's own individual existence from all others by its finitude. One's life is separable from others; it has its own beginning and its own ending. But, because of that separation, one can be an integrated whole — a being with its own unique past, present, and future. Narrative thus provides the opportunity for the individual to make existential sense of mortality, and, correlatively, through the narrative, the profound experience of mortality becomes sociologically accessible.

Autobiographies by historical, popular, and literary figures are a well-established genre. Anthropologists have customarily written autobiographical statements — tales of the field — in the margins of their ethnographies or as separate books (for a review of these, see Van Maanen, 1988). Although contemporary sensibilities question the purposes and veracity of these tales, especially as they inscribe the ethnographer as the knower and the culture of the other as the known, they are exemplars of ethnographers making autobiographical sense of their own lived experience. More recently, sociologists have begun writing autobiographies, writing narratives about sociology, as they write narratives about themselves (see Ellis, 1989; Linden, 1989; Reinharz, 1979; Riley, 1988).

Biography

Third, because people can narrativize their own lives, the possibility arises of understanding other people's lives as likewise biographically organized. Social and generational cohesion, as well as social change, depend upon this ability to empathize with the life stories of others. Social interaction depends upon actors making sense of others' actions and motivations from the *point of view* of the others, from their biographical perspective. Social cooperation relies upon this human capability, a capability grounded in narrative. But the ability to understand another's biography goes beyond creating an interactionally presently shared world: it makes possible the understanding of people who are not present. Narrative creates the possibility of history beyond the personal. Contemporaries, predecessors, and successors communicate through the narrative (Schutz, 1962). Passing on the biographies of heroes and villains links the generations and shapes the disorderly and chaotic, or boring and repetitive, into a communally shared world of experience. Through the communication of the past to present listeners, contemporary worlds are enlarged and grounded. Social scientists are now adding to the bounty of biographies written by historians, journalists, literary biographers, and factual-fictionists (see Deegan, 1988; Stewart, 1989).

The Cultural Story

The cultural story is the fourth way in which narrative is sociologically significant. Participation in a culture includes participation in the narratives of that culture, a general understanding of the stock of meanings and their relationships to each other. The process of telling the story creates and supports a social world. Cultural stories provide exemplars of lives, heroes, villains, and fools as they are embedded in larger cultural and social frameworks as well as stories about home, community, society, and humankind. Morality and cautionary tales instruct the young, control the adult. Stories of one's people—as chosen or enslaved, conquerors or victims—as well as stories about one's nation, social class, gender, race, occupation, etc. affect morale, aspirations, and personal life chances. These are not simply stories but are narratives that have real consequences for the fates of individuals, communities, and nations (see McClelland, 1961).

The cultural story is told from the point of view of the ruling interests and the normative order, and it bears a narrative kinship to functionalism. Since, for example, the central character in a patriarchal system is the male, a cultural story of adultery is about the normative status, marriage, and how another woman tries to ruin a family by stealing a man from his wife. The central character in this story is the husband, and the storyline blames the minor characters, the women: the wife, for her deficient sexiness/lovingness/understandingness; the other woman, for her deficient morality. This particular cultural story, in the United States, transcends race and class lines, making it seem true and giving it a hold on the imaginations of men and women. Cultural stories, thus, help maintain the status quo.

The Collective Story

There is, however, a fifth kind of narrative that gives voice to those who are silenced or marginalized in the cultural narrative. I call this narrative the *collective story.* The collective story displays an individual's story by narrativizing the experiences of the social category to which the individual belongs, rather than by telling the particular individual's story or by simply retelling the cultural story (see Richardson, 1988a). There is a multitude of collective stories in contemporary society. Some of the collective stories arise through social movement activity, such as the civil rights movements, which resist the cultural narratives about groups of people and tell alternative stories. But other collective stories are about people who are not collectively organized. For example, there is the "new other woman" collective story (Richardson, 1985), which takes the point of view of the single woman. In this collective story, the single woman is not cast as a villain in the marriage plot, in combat with another woman over having the love of a man. Rather, she is the central character in her own drama, struggling with old cultural plots and new possibilities of economic and emotional independence for women. Similarly, there are the cancer survivor, battered wife, abused child, coming out, alcoholic, diabetes, chronic illness, codependent, and divorce narratives, to name but a few (see Denzin, 1987; Ferraro and Johnson, 1983; Maines, 1989). Although the narrative is about a category of people, the individual response to the well-told collective story is, "That's *my* story. I am not alone."

Most significant are the transformative possibilities of the collective story. At the individual level, people make sense of their lives through the stories that are available to them, and they attempt to fit their lives into the available stories. People live by stories. If the available narrative is limiting, destructive, or at odds with the actual life, peoples' lives end up being limited and textually disenfranchised. Collective stories that deviate from standard cultural plots provide new narratives; hearing them legitimates replotting one's own life. New narratives offer the patterns for new lives. The story of the transformed life, then, becomes a part of the cultural heritage affecting future stories, future lives.

Transformative possibilities of the collective story also exist at the sociocultural level. People who belong to a particular category can develop a consciousness of kind and can galvanize other category members through the telling of the collective story. People do not even have to know each other for the social identification to take hold. By emotionally binding together people who have had the same experiences, whether in touch with each other or not, the collective story overcomes some of the isolation and alienation of contemporary life. It provides a sociological community, the linking of separate individuals into a shared consciousness. Once linked, the possibility for social action on behalf of the collective is present, and, therewith, the possibility of societal transformation.

Writing, therefore, if not an isolated or purely academic activity. Rather, writing is an ethical "authority" problem as well, an issue to which I now turn.

5. AUTHORITY AND AUTHORSHIP

Because writing is always value constituting, there are always the problems of authority and authorship. Writing narratives does not overcome these problems any more than does logico-scientific writing. Narrative explanation, in practice, means that one person's voice — the writer's — speaks for that of others. In social science writing, narrators often speak about and for constituencies to which they do not belong. These practices, of course, raise postmodernist issues about the researcher's authority and privilege. For

whom do we speak and to whom do we speak, with what voi   ·
using what criteria?

These writing issues are of concern, even when the te:
ostensibly disenfranchised speakers, because wherever text is being produced there is the question of what social, power, and sexual relationships of
production are being *reproduced.* How does our writing reproduce a system
of domination, and how does it challenge that system? What right do we have
to speak for others? to write their lives?

But what are the alternatives? To propose the stilling of the sociologist-
writer's voice not only rejects the value of sociological insight but implies
that somehow facts exist without interpretation. This presupposes a belief in
essences and authenticity, a view that carries its own metaphysical and
political baggage. Accordingly, "there is no principled resolution, no alternative, to the problem of speaking for others. There is no getting it right about
who or what another is; there is no essence defining what 'right' is" (Roth,
1989, p. 31). However we choose to write, we are involved in intentional
behavior, and intentional behavior is a site of moral responsibility. Further,
because power differences are always being played out in personal and civic
arenas, there is no way to avoid deploying one's power if one chooses to
act/write in this world.

What is necessary, I think, is a merging of progressive and postmodernist
thinking about authors and authority. The progressive impulse is to give voice
to those who have been silenced, to speak for others — even constituencies to
which one may not belong. On the other hand, the postmodernist impulse has
been to delete the author, to dismantle distinctions between fact and fiction,
and to deconstruct the difference between sign and signified (or the construction of the ultimate metaphor, where nothing "is" itself). As the speechless
are given voice and the power to name and be named through progressive
writing, the postmodernist theorist would disempower them by erasing their
names, deconstructing their stories, undermining their ground for authority.
A progressive-postmodernist rewriting, however, proposes that, because all
knowledge is partial and situated, it does not mean that there is no knowledge
or that situated knowledge is bad. There is no view from "nowhere," the
authorless text. There is no view from "everywhere," except for God. There
is only a view from "somewhere," an embodied, historically and culturally
situated speaker (Haraway, 1988).

From this perspective, the sociologist speaks as a narrator, a person with
a point of view; an embodied person responsible for his or her words. And
the metanarrative that drives postmodernism is revealed as just that — another

narrative, another point of view. Rather than decrying our sociohistorical limitations, then, we can use that specificity to ask relevant (useful, empowering, enlightening) questions. Consequently, the most pressing issue, as I see it, is a practical-ethical one: how should we use our skills and privileges?

Telling collective stories is one way in which we as social scientists can use our skills and privileges to give voice to those whose narratives have been excluded from the public domain and civic discourse. Writing collective stories enlists our sociological imagination, as we convert private problems into public issues, thereby making collective identity, and collective solutions possible. Writing narratively permits us to tell collective stories as *both* true *and* partial.

But before collective stories can be told, they have to be discovered. Sociological discovery, generally, happens through finding out about people's lives from the people themselves — listening to how people experience their lives and frame their worlds, working inductively, rather than deductively. Qualitative researchers, generally, learn about other people through interaction in specified roles, such as participant observer/informant, interviewee/interviewer, and so on. As a result, their knowledge of people's lives is always historically and temporally grounded. Most ethnographers are keenly aware that knowledge of the world they enter is partial, situated, and subjective knowledge.

Partiality and subjectivity, however, are not the research and writing disadvantages that positivist empiricism proposes. Because knowledge is always partial, limited, and contextual, there is no escape from subjectivity. Subjectivity is constructed in specific contexts; it is not eternally fixed. Qualitative researchers can more comfortably than positivist empiricists adapt to a postmodernist epistemology. As qualitative researchers, we can more easily write as situated, positioned authors, giving up, if we choose, our *authority* over the people we study, but not the responsibility of *authorship* of our texts.

The writing of substantive (data-based) texts, however, is different from writing about writing texts. How subjects are inscribed, who the audience is, what rhetorical and literary tropes are deployed to what effect, when and why — these are not only theoretical and ethical problems but very real, practical ones. If the practical writing problems cannot be resolved, then obviously writers cannot write. I turn now to practical problems and writing strategies for shaping qualitative research into texts for different kinds of readers — trade, professional, and mass circulation.

PART II

Practical Solutions

In what follows, I write about my own substantive writing, seeing my work, now, quite differently than when I wrote it. Many rhetorical and literary elements were present in my writing, some consciously, some only semiconsciously, not named or wholly analyzed. Some of these devices worked well, others not so well. Thus the following analytical discussion "re-visions" my writing process, and, as the account is more personal, the tone of this manuscript changes somewhat. "I" am more present as a speaker and a subject. My hope is that the analysis will help the reader "vision" and "revision" their own and future texts. But, before I discuss concrete writing problems, I want to tell you something about the research upon which the writing depended.

6. DISCOVERING A COLLECTIVE STORY

Over a period of eight years, I interviewed 65 single women who were involved in long-term (over a year) relationships with married men. Their accounts challenged the cultural stereotypes of the other woman as psychopathic, immature, and unfeminist, stereotypes that I, too, held and brought with me into the project. Demographic, sociological, and cultural levels dovetailed with the women's accounts of their lives.

In a society where there was a demographic paucity of eligible men, but where a woman's self-esteem was still dependent upon having the love of a man, and in a society where women were urged to achieve autonomy, career success, and sexual fulfillment, but where they were still expected to put their lovers' needs above their own, the tension between achieving both an independent identity and a satisfying intimate relationship was severe. One solution to the contradictory messages was a liaison with a married man. Because 34 million single women in the United States are constrained by the same demographic and cultural realities, being involved with a married man is a ubiquitous social phenomenon. Psychological or psychopathological explanations are inadequate and cannot explain the burgeoning social fact of single woman/married man liaisons.

Because individual women are subject to the same social, cultural, and demographic forces, and because the individual stories of the single women were similarly contoured, I began to think of these woman as a *social* category, the *Other Woman.* Believing that their liaisons would be temporary, these women imagined they would achieve intimacy in them without sacrificing independence. However, because of the relationship's secrecy in conjunction with overarching gender inequalities, the woman often ended up caring for her lover more than she had intended. The more she cared about him, the more dependent and less powerful she became, because she carried into the relationship the normative expectations of women in love — personal sacrifice. The particulars of the stories were different, and there were different subplots, but the main thematic was the same.

I had "discovered" the Other Woman "collective story," an historically situated story whose theme and plot differs from the established cultural story. Hearing the perspective of the Other Woman, I felt, would help personal, cultural, and social transformative projects by illuminating sources of divisiveness between disempowered groups. I wanted to tell this story to diverse audiences.

I turn now to an ex post facto analysis of how I shaped the interview materials into a trade book, academic articles, and articles for mass circulation.

7. WRITING A TRADE BOOK

My decision to write a trade book evolved over a period of years. The more I pondered the question, "Sociology for whom?" the more certain I felt that sociology should be widely disseminated. Research on the Other Woman had implications, I thought, for the lives of single women, husbands, wives, and adult children of divorced parents. I also wanted the sociological-feminist perspective to frame the book, not the "how-to" or "pop-psych" frame that characterizes mass-market books. As a result, I wanted to write what I thought of as a serious trade book for a respected publishing house.

Fifty thousand books are published each year. Twenty thousand of them are trade books. The trade books compete — along with cards, sweatshirts, calendars, and best-selling mass-market books — for extremely limited shelf space. Each book, moreover, demands individual name recognition by the potential buyer. There is no other consumer industry like it — so many new products (books) from such a large number of producers (publishers) with so few distributors (bookstores) with such little space (bookshelves). Consequently, the competition among trade books is fierce. Most books succumb quickly; a cabbage has a longer shelf life than the average trade book; 90% of trade books are dead, shredded, or remaindered within the year (Shatzkin, 1982).

I did not know any of this when I decided to write a trade book. I naively assumed that if I wrote a good book, publishers would clamor to publish it. At first, I tried to get an agent, but none was interested, because I was (just) a professor who had not yet published a trade book, and because they did not think the topic was of general interest. Then I sent a prospectus, sample chapters, and examples of my academic writing to a dozen publishing houses known for their sociology line. This was the strategy I had used to publish a gender text book; then it had elicited (by what seemed like return mail) a half-dozen actual contracts. But in this case, months passed. Even the presses where I had previously published academic texts did not respond, because, as I learned later, trade and text divisions do not communicate with each other. Eventually, two presses answered negatively; I have yet to hear from nine others. But late one evening (when I least expected it), Joyce Seltzer, Senior Editor for the Free Press, telephoned to say that, due to a canceled appointment, she had had some unexpected free time and had picked up my materials, which had been on her desk for several months. The material, she said, was "riveting," but I would have to frame and write it differently if they were to publish it. She was willing, she said, to help me with this process.

Luck, thus, played a major role in my writing of a trade book. But, if I were to do it again, I would try even harder to get an agent, especially if I were interested in a large trade publishing house (e.g., Knopf or Simon & Schuster.) I might take a course in trade publishing, read books about the process (see Powell, 1985), and talk with experienced colleagues. In any case, I would want the book to be sponsored and recommended to a specific editor by an agent, sales representative, acquisitions editor, or a colleague who had published with that editor or reviewed for her/him.

In part due to good fortune, patience, and a willingness to adapt, then, my not-yet-written manuscript went into contract with the Free Press. However, because I wanted the book to appeal to both lay and professional audiences and to have a liberatory effect upon its readers, how to write it entailed thinking about and experimenting with different literary and rhetorical devices. In what follows, I address five major devices that shaped *The New Other Woman:* encoding, narrative stance, tone, quotations and biographical narratives, and synecdoche. Again, my comments are not offered as "shoulds" but as one set of strategies to the problems presented by trade books. I underscore that much of my understanding of what I did, I only understand now, after the fact, through reconstructionist lenses.

Encoding

All writing is *encoded,* serving the rhetorical function of locating it in a particular genre, helping the reader to know what to expect, and thereby, in actuality, helping the writer, who can then draw upon the habits of thought, glosses, and specialized knowledge of the reader. Audiences have expectations regarding "their" texts. Overall organization, code words, title, authorial designation, metaphors, images, and so on serve as signposts to potential readers. When the audiences for the same book are diverse or discrete, the writing problem becomes more complex and important, because the text has simultaneously to reach differing readerly sensibilities. Three major encodings are trade, academic, and moral/political perspective.

In general, trade encoding is accomplished through such literary devices as jazzy titles, attractive covers, lack of specialized jargon, marginalization of methodology, common-world metaphors and images, and book blurbs and prefatory material about the "lay" interest in the material. Academic encoding is accomplished through such literary devices as prominent display of academic credentials of author, references, footnotes, methodology sections, use of familiar academic metaphors and images (such as "exchange theory," "roles," and "stratification"), and book blurbs and prefatory material about the science or scholarship involved. The moral/political perspective is encoded through such literary devices as in-group words in the title, for example, woman/women/feminist in feminist writing; the moral or activist "credentials" of the author, for example, the author's role in particular social movements; references to moral and activist authorities; empowerment metaphors; and book blurbs and prefatory material about how this work relates to real people's lives. Other writing genres are similarly encoded. Problems with writing books that transcend genres begin with deciding which of the potentially conflicting encoding conventions to deploy when. The book I wrote deployed encoding from trade, academic, and a particular moral/political perspective, feminism. I turn to these encodings now.

TRADE ENCODING

Under standard contract agreements, authors have no control over the title or the cover of their books. The title (*The New Other Woman: Contemporary Single Women in Affairs with Married Men*) and the cover (a five-color, highly graphic profile of a woman's face with bright red lips and red earring, her eyes covered by a wide brimmed hat) were jointly proposed by the publicity and art directors and are exemplars of trade encoding. My objections that the title shunted aside the enduring sociological value of the work were ignored because marketing considerations had primacy. The book would be marketed as a trade book under the campaign of "What's New?" (For a description and analysis of book tours, see Richardson, 1987). Similarly, trade encoding dominated the overall formal structure of the book. Methodological concerns were marginalized, placed in the preface and appendix; chapters were kept short; and section headings in chapters, such as one finds in texts, academic papers, and mass-market how-to's were absent. The book, then, looks like a serious trade book, rather than an academic or a mass-market book.

Although an author can argue with the editor and staff about the look of the book, the author is unlikely to win the argument(s). In a trade house, a corps of publicity and marketing specialists lay claim to expertise and experience beyond that of the author's. Editors defer to the specialists. The author, I think, is wise to avoid alienating the marketing staff, because the author is, finally, dependent upon the staff's goodwill. Behind every (successful and unsuccessful) book, there are social practices and interpersonal relationships that have produced it. One thing you can do to help the staff help you is to complete the questionnaire sent to authors regarding marketing, provide a long list of people who should know about your book, and, submit some ideas and examples of press copy and blurbs for your book. (For more information about working with the publicity departments, see Powell, 1985; Richardson, 1987.)

ACADEMIC ENCODING

Because trade publishers control the design and marketing of your book, however, the academic author's problems with encoding the book as an academic one are magnified. If the book has topical, deviant, or "sexy" content — as many qualitative researchers' books do — the encoding becomes even more important, because the tendency among book readers and book reviewers, who are interested in works with ostensibly enduring qualities or who do not wish to be associated with the topic in question, is to dismiss the book as *not* scholarly.

Encoding a trade book as also an academic one is less of a writerly problem if the book is published with a university press, which signals its scholarly pedigree with its imprimatur. Although university presses are now publishing manuscripts that have a trade potential, by using in-house publicity and design staffs to encode books as trade, marketing them to lay audiences, and, sometimes, selling the paperback rights to regular trade houses, the university sponsorship of its publication pretty much guarantees its professional legitimacy.

I encoded *The New Other Woman* as an academic book through a number of rhetorical devices. Chief among them is the overall *organization* of the book, spelled out in the table of contents: preface, acknowledgments, chapters with titles, appendix, footnotes, bibliography, and index. These are book parts that academics expect. Second are a variety of *appeals to* sociological *legitimacy.* The academic reader who looks at books from the opening pages, finds standard cues about sample, methods, validity, reliability, scope, and the author's claim to be writing for a professional audience, as well as a lay one. Those who start at the end find ten pages of bibliography (maybe even a reference to themselves) and a four-page interview guide. And those who "graze" the text find sociology's concepts and theories, page after page. I am continuously establishing the work as sociology, not psychology (which was the category designated by the publisher, because psychology has a better "market" than sociology). Words such as *demographic, cultural, society, role,* and *social movements,* for example, pepper the text, resonate with social scientists, but are not thought of as jargon by lay readers. Buried beneath the apparent "plain speak" are metaphoric, theoretical, and empirical traditions, which position and deepen the text for the social scientist. For example, the argument of the first chapter that "Other Womanhood" is a major social phenomenon draws upon demographic analyses, dual labor market analyses, gender analysis, exchange theory, labeling theory, reference group theory,

Durkheimian functionalism, Merton's theory of anomie, latent consequences analysis, and social movement theory. Although most of these are not labeled in the text, they become the important sociological *subtext* of the book and the basis upon which I lay claim to an enduring sociological interest.

FEMINIST ENCODING

The third encoding problem for me was to signal the book as a feminist book, but to do so in such a way as also to invite nonfeminists to read it. This was primarily accomplished through the use of bland *code words* such as "woman" and "women" in the title, rather than "feminist" or "patriarchy," for example, and identification of myself as a "researcher in gender," rather than as a "feminist activist." "Voices" is another important feminist code word. Potential readers were told in the blurb and shown if they riffled the pages that herein they would find the "voices" of women telling their "own stories" in their "own words." "Validity," according to the preface, "finally" rests in whether the analysis "resonates with the experiences" of women. The opening sentence of the Preface, "A friend had been an other woman . . .," and the last sentence of the book, ". . . what modern women are looking for: freedom and security," code the book as a "woman's book."

Encoding, though, is just the surface strategy of trade book writing. I turn, now, to the problem of narrative stance.

Narrative Stance

There are several well-established narrative stances, as well as some newly emergent ones, within the qualitative writing tradition. There is no single right stance. What works for one author at one time may not work for other authors or the same author at a different time. Choice will depend upon one's skills, dispositions, aesthetic preferences, and personal and political goals. The problem of finding one's own narrative voice, however, is prerequisite and central.

In writing *The New Other Woman,* I considered a number of different narrative stances before settling on one. I declined the ethnographic verité style, the publication of (cleaned-up) interview transcripts, because it requires the reader, rather than the writer, to make sociological sense of the material. I also rejected the biographical case, such as is found in the writings of Oscar Lewis and Studs Terkel, because however successful such productions are as literature, few succeed as social science. Similarly, I ruled out the paraphrasing or facsimile style (e.g., found in some of Lillian Rubin's work) because it makes the different interviewees sound alike, and like the narrator. I also avoided experimental writing in which, for example, pages are split, giving simultaneous voice to researcher and respondent, or personifying different aspects of the research process (e.g., having the text dialogue with the author), because my intentions were to write substantive book *content,* rather than draw attention to the *writing.* With a topic such as mine, conventional format could conceal radical content.

Consequently, I experimented in a more mundane way, writing several of the women's stories as scenes. I described the setting, established the ambience, the interactions, created the characters, and wrote the interview up as a scene between the Other Woman and myself. The women had fictitious names, which revealed their narrative essence. "Lisa Maxwell" used her liaison to get a new *lease* on life by changing careers, a change that was of *maximal* value to her. "Michelle Mitchell" was highly narcissistic, experimenting with "masculine" and "feminine" roles. Being an Other Woman was part of the experiment. "Abby Goodman" was a psychologist who prided herself on her listening skills, her kindness, and her hospitality. She was duped by her lover. Each woman had her own story, her own chapter, her own analysis. I felt powerful. I felt like a "writer."

But this narrative voice did not work. The format implied that each story represented something different *sociologically.* Because each story was separately analyzed, I was, in fact, writing individual sociobiographies, rather than what I wanted to write, a *collective story.* Secondly, I felt that I was seriously treading into the genre of fiction — not just using literary techniques — and that neither did my skills as a writer warrant such a venture, nor, finally, would my sociological and political purposes be served by my attempts to reconstruct the sociological interview as realist fiction.

Although the differences between fiction and science break down in contemporary thinking, they are not totally demolished. Science still requires, for example, appeals to credibility and verisimilitude to work as science; the science writer still intends his work to be read (judged, evaluated) as research, not as a fictional account. The science writer with explicit moral positions, especially, I think, needs to write texts as credible research, rather than as the result of an active imagination, so that the intended political and ethical content of the work has some chance of entering the social consciousness.

Finally, I decided to shape the material by interlocking two story lines or narratives: a social-scientific analytic one and the Other Woman's collective story. In the process, "I" disappeared, partly because my editor, preferring the authority engendered through the science writing model, wanted it that way, and partly because there was no writerly place for me in the stories I was writing. Writing myself explicitly into the text would detract from my political and research goals, on the one hand, but writing myself out of the text meant I was assuming the authority to write about others, to tell their lives as an omniscient narrator, occupying a godlike position, safely distanced from the people on my pages. I opted for omniscience, tempered with the decision to use literary techniques that would decenter my authority. I shall return to this problem, later, when I discuss tone.

ANALYTICAL CHRONOLOGIES

Two interlocked narratives drive the book: a sociological narrative and the Other Woman's collective story. For want of a better term, I call them analytical chronologies. The sociologist's narrative brackets the Other Woman's narrative. The first chapter tells a sociologist's story about the society in which we live, its history and attitudes toward single women involved with married men, and the contemporary social and demographic conditions currently affecting these women, while the final chapter projects how lives would/could be lived in the future. The second narrative, the Other Woman's collective story, is the book's centerpiece and is built from the words and lives of the women I interviewed. It is their story(ies) that I was trying to tell and their voices I wanted heard. But because I wanted the sociologist's narrative and the Other Woman's collective story to be interlinked, the sociological narrator appears in the Other Woman's chapters, and their lives appear in the first and last bracketing chapters, rather than adapting the social scientific writing convention of separating data from theory and implications.

The Other Woman's collective story begins with her life prior to her involvement, and then moves chronologically from meeting the married man, to getting involved, having sex, falling in love, concealing the relationship, dealing with his wife, feeling bad, and ending the liaison. The material fit almost naturally into a plot, with events making sense in the context of their consequences and with the reader not quite sure what the next chapter would bring. I did not, so to speak, spill the beans in the introduction. Rather, I had purloined the powerful literary device of the mystery story in writing the book. I wanted readers to wonder, "And then what? And then?" Chapter endings forewarned plot twists, but not specifics. I wanted readers to be surprised by the outcomes, but convinced by the evidence, elements found in successfully constructed mysteries. I wanted everything in retrospect to seem inevitable.

One of the chapters in the book, however, "His Wife," did not fit into the chronological sequence as neatly as the chapters that focused on the *process* of intimacy construction between the principals, the single woman and the married man — just as a chapter on the Other Woman might not fit neatly into the chronological story of a dissolved marriage. Yet, the wife was a character in every Other Woman's story, sometimes offstage and minor, and sometimes center stage and major. Further, readers' (and editors') expectations, as well as my own political concern with easing tensions between women, demanded that I write about wives. Consequently, I made a narrative decision to interrupt the plot, but not the *points of view.* The narratives were still told from the perspectives of the Other Woman and the sociological narrator, not the wife. This brings us to the problem of tone.

Tone

Taking the narrative stance of omniscience raised the major poststructuralist question about authority. This question is a double-barreled one: Do researchers have the right to speak for others, distancing themselves from the text, acting as if their own subjectivity were not being inscribed in the text? And, conversely, how can the credibility of the writer's claims to knowledge be decided? There are no philosophical resolutions to these problems, however, as discussed earlier, because one can never *be* another, because who the other "is" is in continuous flux and change, anyway, and because there is no "final authority" on authority. Some people, nevertheless have greater access to skills, knowledge, resources, and publishing houses than others, and, therewith are accorded greater authority, by themselves and others. If those with privileged access speak only for themselves, the voices of those less privileged have no chance of textual enfranchisement.

Given an overarching inequitable sociohistorical context, those of us with privileged access to writing lives and who desire a more equitable social world, do, however, have a principled resolution to the authority problem, a resolution, I think, we can live with as moral actors in a postmodernist climate. Writing is a *moral* site. Any moral site is a site of *intentionality.* We can choose to write so that the voice of those we write about is respected, strong and true. Ironically, this kind of writing also contributes to the credibility of our own interpretive voice. Stated this way, writing strategies are not just literary or scientific choices: they are moral decisions.

One of the most important and least talked about literary ways in which the author's intentions are realized is *tone,* because tone reveals the implicit moral attitude of the writer toward the material. My attitude toward my material, finally, was how *normal* Other Women were—how like other women they were, how their lives could be Anywoman's, Everywoman's.

Tone is revealed in many different ways, such as choice of metaphors, organization of material, how a quotation or a person's experience is framed and treated by the narrator, what and how much the narrator lets who say and so on. Tone, consequently, becomes a way for the omniscient writers of qualitative research to accomplish two interlocking tasks: reduction of their authority over writing for others, and amplification of their credibility as writers of interpretive social science.

In *The New Other Woman,* readers hear for themselves the Other Women's voices, and they hear the sociological analysis. This helps establish the tone of the book as one of fairness and reasonableness. Providing the evidence, the words and experiences of the single women, places the book within the social science frame, encoding methods of data gathering and analysis. The women's voices bring the reader back to the lives of individual women, whereas the sociological analysis frames those lives. This tonal-textual staging simultaneously increases the women's presence as speakers and my credibility as an interpreter, because I have decentered myself as the final authority.

Structuring Quotations and Biographical Narratives

Deciding how to present voices and lives is a continuous problem for qualitative writers. Because we use the voices and experiences of the people we study, both for their own sake and as evidence of our credibility, we are constantly making writerly decisions about who gets to say what and how and how often in the text, and who the narrator talks about, how and how often. How do you write the voices and lives of interviewees and informants so that both literary and science writing criteria are met? This is not an either/or problem. Qualitative books are often critiqued as bad science, not because they necessarily are, but because the *literary* decisions regarding presentation of lives are busily undermining the work's credibility.

One of the primary ways to meet both literary and science writing criteria is through variety in format and voice. You can use one-line quotations, sometimes standing by themselves, sometimes in droves; mid-length quotations (5-10 lines) by themselves or mixed with one-liners; short phrases quoted within the body of the narrative; long(er) quotations broken into paragraphs, deployed when the reader cares about the character or the topic; and episodes, ministories embedded within the larger narrative. Similarly, including quotes with a variety of language patterns, images, slang, and regionalisms makes texts both more alive and more credible.

However one structures the text, though, the first problem for qualitative researchers is to convince the reader to read the evidence, the quotations, and biographical details. Because readers tend to skip over indented passages, particularly those in fine print and those that seem to go on and on and on, it is preferable for quotations to be typeset like the text, and important that your interpretive work — the lead-ins and lead-outs around the quotations — entice.

SHORT QUOTATIONS AND BIOGRAPHICAL EVENTS

Readers are more likely to read short, eye-catching quotations. It is important that these short quotations be especially worthy of the reader's attention, beginning with the most important of all the quotes, the first ones in the text. This is where you earn, or lose, the trust of the reader.

The first quotes in *The New Other Woman* appear on the first page of the women's story of getting involved. After stating that "most Other Women explicitly deny premeditation," four women speak:

> I would never calculate to have an affair with a married man. I never intended to get involved.

> I was into my celibate period. I wasn't interested in men, much less a married one.

> After my husband left me for an other woman, I told myself I would never, never do that to another woman. (pp. 13-14)

The content and format of the quotes accomplish several tasks. They are short and easy to read; they stand out from the narrator's text but verify it; they say something unexpected and surprising; they write against normative definitions; the speaking "I" of an individual is privileged; diversity within generality is modeled; each voice is different in style and content; and no one is special pleading, so the Other Women have a chance of being heard, perhaps even understood and liked. Following these quotations, I propose their generality, but qualify their universality, and introduce what will become the chapter's theme:

The theme [of explicit denial of premeditation] is so persistent that it cannot be dismissed: single women, by and large, do not see themselves as husband poachers. (p. 14)

Short quotations are a valuable rhetorical device, moreover, throughout a text. Piling up indented short quotations illustrates diversity within sameness, without diverting the reader to side topics. For example, after discussing how, prior to their liaisons, single women were going through different kinds of transitions, I briefly quote from five different women:

I was returning to school after a five-year hiatus. I was nervous and excited.

My husband had left me for another woman, and I was struggling to get my self-esteem back.

I was just starting out as a lawyer.

I wanted to find out who I was.

I was working out whether I could be heterosexual or not. (pp. 16-17)

Five major kinds of sociological transitions — education, marital, occupational, existential, and sexual orientation — are represented in the quotations. Each quote matters. The short quotes open up the text to institutional and lived-experience diversity, but they do not disengage the reader from the unfolding narrative. If I had quoted at *length* the experiences of women in transition, the book could have lost its focus, its story diverted into a different, albeit also interesting, story of Women in Transition.

EMBEDDED QUOTATIONS

Embedding brief quoted phrases within the analyst's narrative rivets the readers' attention on analysis. Embedding is an especially strong rhetorical device on two different occasions. First, it is to prepare a reader for a shift in emphasis. This is exemplified in the following excerpt, which follows several pages of discussion of the Other Woman's denial of culpability toward "his wife":

42

As the relationship progresses, specific kinds of guilt feelings can emerge such as "spending his wife's money," "keeping him away from the kids," "changing him," or volitionally "staying" in the relationship. One way to deny those blameworthy feelings is to *deny that his wife exists.* (p. 90)

The sources of guilt differ from what readers might expect, reflect different speakers, and open the text to the next major section — ways in which single women cope with the other woman in their lover's life, his wife.

A second rhetorical occasion for embedding quotes is when the point is a minor one; embedding displays the point and allows you to move on, as shown below:

Single women cast married men into the role of *old friend* or *new friend.* Old friends are familiar and safe. For example, a woman who had known her eventual married lover since college thought it "only natural" that he should "help" her do the "heavy work around the house" following her divorce. After he had "cleaned the gutters" or "mowed the lawn," they would "eat lunch and drink beer," and "talk about old times." "Real good friends." (p. 29)

"Old friends" is a minor point, but the concrete details of the budding liaison between the quoted woman and her "old friend" make good reading when embedded as a minibiographical narrative, much more so than if the whole story were quoted in its entirety. The details ring true. Readers can see the old friends eating, drinking, talking; they get an inkling of how, as another woman phrased it, "friends turn into lovers," which is a major theme of the book.

LONGER QUOTATIONS

To communicate more complex sociological understandings, longer passages and/or more extensive biographical details are called for. Choosing an example that is simultaneously pedestrian and extraordinary, I think, strengthens the argument. To show how people who had not even seen each other could become illicit lovers, I quote from a woman editor who communicated initially with her eventual married lover, a writer, only through the computer:

I met him on-line. We worked together through computer conferencing. I liked how his mind worked . . . Then one day he called me [on the computer] on the personal mode — that way no one else could read the message. I was flattered that he approached me because I had this mental picture of him as someone important. So we started chatting on-line. I thought an electonic flirtation would be safe. (p. 19)

The reader *sees* the sociological understanding, the deeply entrenched heterosexual eroticism of the society. No amount of telling the reader works as well as showing.

When differences are central to understanding the complexity of the narrative — how different subplots lead to the same conclusion — more biographical detail and more and longer quotes are probably called for. For example, having sex with a married man allowed the women to explore their sexuality in two seemingly contradictory ways: less repression, for some women, and more reticence, for others. About one woman, I write:

For one overweight woman whose mother had told her she was ugly, unwanted, unlovable, and boring, even to her therapist, a relationship with a married man helped her overcome her sexual fears. (p. 44)

I follow this lead-in with a longish quotation from her:

My weight problem was a way of defending myself against being a sexual person. I had been overweight my entire life and have felt tremendously insecure about my sexuality. Food was partly a substitute for sex, and my weight kept me out of circulation — or had me believe I was out of circulation. My weight didn't matter to him [married lover] and I found I could let go with him because I knew it wasn't going anywhere. (p. 45)

Three other women, who were released from family rigidity or personal fear regarding sexuality are biographically described and quoted. These women are then contrasted to women who find that they can restrict their sexual lives, if they choose, more easily if involved with a married man. Two examples follow:

Because he was married, I didn't have to sleep with him a lot, but it was important to me to sleep with him because it was one of the ways I concealed to myself that I was a lesbian. I could say to myself I was still sleeping with men . . . Single men . . . [thought] that once they slept with you . . . you had no right to [ever] say no.

Single guys think you owe them sex because they're so nice to go out with you. Yuck. There's this whole thing with the male shortage or something and single men think they're just so swell to date you. The pits. (p.47)

Biographical details and quotations resolve the apparent paradox: sex with married men gives single women greater control over their sexual lives than sex with single, available, men.

When writing against received wisdom, it is rhetorically and scientifically important to show how your data contradict that wisdom. Whenever, for example, I found evidence that an Other Woman fit the cultural stereotype, I talked about it from both her perspective and mine, as narrator. This meant more biographical details and longer quotes, because the arguments were more complex. The second chapter, for example, concludes with a four-page description and analysis of two women, who ostensibly contradict the thesis of the chapter, the unintentionality of getting involved, but who, finally, illustrate the difficulty women, of all kinds and dispositions, have in controlling who they fall in love with when.

THEMATIC BIOGRAPHICAL NARRATIVES

Denial is a recurrent theme of the book, as it is in women's lives, generally. Throughout the text longer quotes and biographical details from various women's lives are presented illustrating the complexity of that theme. But I also keep returning in different chapters to the lives of particular women who exemplify the theme especially well. One of those women was an attractive young executive who had been hired into a managerial position without the requisite education or experience. She subsequently had a seven-year liaison with the man who hired her, her married supervisor. I begin her story as an example of the tendency of women to deny the impact of sexuality in their working relationships with men. She states:

Occasionally, our whole unit would go for drinks or something, but it was all of us as a group. Then, I became senior manager in the office, and I started having business lunches with him. Those were very professional, if anything, overly so. But the group, still, would go out and socialize at Shadows [a disco]. He and I would talk and dance. After a while, he'd call and say, "Come over to Shadows and we can play backgammon and discuss. . . ." For me, it was like one more male mentor. (p. 26)

I quote at length to give the reader a sense of how this woman defined the situation as ordinary, sociable, and professional. She cast her boss into a pragmatic and morally acceptable role, male mentor. How many other single women make the same assumptions? The tone of the quote is matter-of-fact; the content, from the woman's perspective, mundane. I follow this quote, with the following paragraph:

Socializing with her boss began easily, harmlessly, as the whole unit went together. Twosome business lunches followed, as well as continued group socializing, discos, and dancing. She insisted, however, that his interest, at that point, was only in her executive potential. She refused to acknowledge that a disco was an odd setting for business discussions. "He chose it," she said, "because he knew it was close to my apartment," as though that were a business decision on his part, rather than, as it turned out, "a sexually opportunistic one." (p. 26)

In this paragraph, several things are accomplished. First, the highlights of the indented quote are briefly reiterated, just in case the reader skipped over it. Second, the sociological narrator's voice appears as a skeptical voice, signaled through such phrases as "she refused to acknowledge," "odd setting," and "as though." The narrator does not cast doubt on the veracity of the woman's account, but uses the account to illustrate the woman's capacity for denial. Even though she has recognized that he was "sexually opportunistic," she still denies the relevance of earlier "group socializing, discos, and dancing." Third, by embedding quotes in the narrator's paragraph, there is a dramatic tension between the two voices, reminiscent of the tension that grew between the lovers.

We pick up the young executive's story a page later, following a discussion of how sex with an old friend or workmate can be rationalized by defining it as a temporary aberration. She says:

One night we went out and either I was vulnerable or I don't know what, but he ended up coming back to my place. He didn't stay overnight but called the next morning. It was like, "Are you okay?" The perfect gentleman. And we talked at length about how this might affect work and I said, "If anything, let's just call it a fluke. We were both a little looped." I'm not a one-night stand kind of person, but I felt pretty good about saying that's what happened, because the job was what mattered. (p. 28)

The reader is already familiar with this woman's life and the narrator's point-of-view around these events, so little needs to be said specifically about her perceptions. The lead-out paragraph, rather, is an analytical summary, restating a general theme:

If work or friendship is what really matters, casting him into the temporary role of one-night stand lets the woman hold onto her original definition of the situation. It allows her to return the relationship back to "normal." (p. 28)

Throughout, the text returns to the young executive's life as a quintessential example of how denial operates and how normalcy is constructed. She appears in the book enjoying her sex life, happily in love, thriving in her career, although increasingly emotionally insecure, until, three years into her relationship with her married boss, she is, "by her standards," physically abused, "slapped around and held and bruised and those kind of things," "beaten up and thrown and all that stuff," because, she believes, he was "uncertain about her commitment to him." Like a traditional abused wife, insecure and self-doubting, she had become more economically and psychologically dependent upon her "boss-lover," unable to break up with him without losing both her lover and her job. As it turned out:

He fired her, and hired another single woman, with whom he subsequently had a relationship. (p. 117)

"Our" Other Woman, though, gets the final word about her lover:

I fantasize two different ways of killing him. One, I'd love to stand in front of him with a gun and point-blank shoot him. Painfully, just shoot him. The other way I'd like to have him die is very slowly, and that's not a physical death. I'd like to ruin him credit-wise, reputation wise, destroy his self esteem. Ruin his life, like he ruined mine. He took everything—my youth, my dreams. You would think someone who lives a life like he does, would die. Would be shot. I read the obits every day. Just to see . . . just to see. (p. 123)

I quote at such length for three strong rhetorical reasons. First, readers of early drafts thought I was being too evenhanded toward the married men, and this young woman's emotional outpouring expresses the deep anger toward them of many of the readers of the book. Second, because we have been following this woman's career through the book, a career that began promisingly before abuse and self-doubt set in, we care about her and are somewhat relieved to hear her externalizing her pain. I had not realized how important this was; in the early draft I had only quoted the "obit" line. And third, I use the quote as a lead-in to the denouement, where I summarize sources of pain, humiliation, and loss—loss of time, self-esteem, and dreams—as normatively constructed experiences for women. This brings us to the major rhetorical thrust of *The New Other Woman.*

Synecdoche

The New Other Woman is written from a particular narrative stance, in a particular tone, with particular encodings, metaphors, images, and the like, all of which are intended to achieve a rhetorical end. I work through a paradox and bring the reader along with me. Despite the societal stereotypes that I held before I began my research and that I imagine my reader holds, I want the reader to conclude, as I did, that the Other Woman is not abnormal, but *exemplifies,* in very important respects, the lives of normal contemporary women. She is not living at the margins of society, but rather at its center. She is not deviant, but typical. She is not simply like regular women, a weak metaphoric argument: She *is* regular women.

To accomplish this rhetorical aim, I write the Other Woman as a *synecdoche.* As described earlier, synecdoche is a powerful rhetorical device through which a part or a person or a type can stand for some kind of whole. The collective story I have constructed is a synecdochical one. Arguing from example, whether through a literary character, an ethnographic situation, an in-depth interview, or an experimental or statistical test is a primary way through which we make sense of the world. What makes synecdoche such a powerful rhetorical device is that it fits both the narrative and the logico-empiricist codes of communication. It works, persuasively, in both codes; it links narrative and conventional social science writing.

The major rhetorical thrust of *The New Other Woman* — that the Other Woman is a Normal Woman — has been hinted at throughout this discussion and appears throughout the text. At the end of the preface, for example, I state:

> The Other Woman's experiences have many parallels with the experiences of women, generally. In learning about Other Woman we learn much about the lives, hopes, and problems of Everywomen. (p. xiii)

Throughout the text the *theme* is *normality*. The Other Woman is ordinary, experiencing the "same stresses, pushes and pulls that 'regular' women experience." She has normative expectations for friendship, intimacy, and love. She has been socialized to hold the same goals and desires as other contemporary women. Her expectations are not unreasonable or odd. What appears to be far out, single women/married men liaisons is normal. Indeed, one understands the normal even better by looking at its supposed breach.

If the rhetorical, literary, and science writing are successful, readers will come to see the Other Woman differently, more compassionately and more understandably. Paradoxically, the more they see the Other Woman as normal, the more empowered all women are to alter the civic discourse about and social opportunities for normal women.

I did not know this would be my conclusion when I began my work. I thought I would be writing about an atypical group of women, about illicit sex and social pathology. Reaching the conclusion of normalcy and typicality, however, in no way implies that these social relationships are unalterable. Rather, the analysis points to sociohistorical construction of relationships, the power of narrative in people's lives, the link between narrative and the human sciences, and, therefore, the desirability of telling the stories of the textually disenfranchised, because through their articulation, personal, cultural, and social change is possible.

8. WRITING ACADEMIC PAPERS

Academic papers are encoded with the same academic codes discussed earlier in the scholarly encoding of *The New Other Woman,* but there are other conventions, as well (e.g., length, focus, narrative stance, etc.). Some of these conventions are probably erroneous and should be avoided, while others, although possibly erroneous, may have to be followed, if the author needs to be published in certain journals.

Depending on how the journal positions itself in the postmodernist world, the would-be writer might be expected to write a realistic description, an hypothesis-generating piece, theory, science, members' accounts, a deconstruction, a reflexive analysis, and so on. Most journals have fairly traditional standards of writing up research, however, and most readers expect those traditional standards to be met. For the writer with postmodernist sensibilities this raises complex representational problems. Rather than trying to spell out all those problems in this section, I am going to look at some ways in which qualitative work can be shaped to meet traditional academic standards, without the author being overwhelmed by feelings of self-annihilation in the process. The problems are rhetorical and writerly ones, such as narrative stance, tone, and metaphor.

One of the most important things for qualitative researchers to bear in mind is that they can write up the same material in different ways. The material is malleable. That is why we call it material. How we shape the material depends upon how far along we are in our research, and who we want to read it, for what reasons. The same material can be shaped into a realist article, a postmodernist one, or some admixture of the two. Writing it one way does not preclude writing it from a different frame. Because collecting qualitative data is labor intensive and much of what is collected does not fit into one article, it makes sense to write a number of different pieces, from different angles at different stages of the project.

In-Progress Papers

Writing is often thought of as writing up final results in the final stages of the research process, a writing model that, coincidentally, fits nicely with the funding model of research, but not with the qualitative research process. Instead, I would suggest writing in-progress papers. Through in-progress writing you lay claim to a research territory, formulate proposals for grants, and improve your self-reflexivity: what is your attitude toward the material? what do you think you know? how are you expressing it? In-progress papers might be academically minor, but *literarily* major because they help you find your frame, tone, narrative stance, metaphors, and audience.

NARRATIVE STANCE

Qualitative writers are frequently told to present their work as exploratory research. The exploratory researcher stance, however, does not serve the interests of the writer or of qualitative research, in general — nor is it an accurate depiction of the intentions of most qualitative research. Exploratory research is a code within empiricist discourse referring to research leading to quantitative research, not research done for its own sake and instead of quantitative work. Dubbing qualitative research exploratory serves the interests of logico-empiricist textbooks and journals, but it diminishes and distorts the qualitative enterprise. When research is framed as exploratory, the message is that the paper is of dubious value, and its findings should not be taken very seriously. The exploratory stance implicitly presents qualitative research as foreplay to the desired big, but nonforthcoming-in-this-paper, statistical climax.

The exploratory stance, although prevalent in in-progress papers, is toxic to the novice researcher because exploratory papers often end up being unpublishable, boring, or both. The meaningfulness of qualitative methodology gets lost because the exploratory stance tends to produce the worst of both qualitative and quantitative writing: undeveloped theoretical material, a dearth of dense description (Denzin, 1989), and a barrage of "baby stats," like percentages and frequency tables.

There are, however, alternative ways to frame research so that the preliminary, open-ended, and in-progress state of the project is not denied, masked, or diminished, but built upon. I discuss two such alternatives: the "typology" and the "continuum." Although these normally require an omniscient narrator, some of the poststructuralist issues surrounding omniscience can be adjudicated in the textual staging.

THE TYPOLOGY

The *typology,* constituting the material in terms of a classification scheme or "types" of *X,* is a powerful rhetorical device that does not undermine your own research or the entire qualitative research enterprise. The purpose of a typology for a qualitative researcher is not the creation of an exhaustive classificatory scheme, which may be the goal of logico-empiricists, but (a) to find *something* in your material worthy of classification and (b) to provide *some* of the categories. This is a modest, worthy, and attainable goal. The first paper I wrote on the "Other Woman," for example, was a typology of how these liaisons ended. The idea of writing about endings was not my own but was in a "Call for Papers" on that topic for a special edition of a highly respected qualitative journal (Richardson, 1979a). (Serendipity, again.) Endings was the "something" worth talking about, and based on my already completed interviews, I could construct three ideal types of endings and provide ample description of them. I did not claim an all-encompassing analysis.

Typologies are excellent rhetorical devices for framing qualitative work, for they can be written with an open-endedness, help the researcher sift through ethnographic materials in a focused way, and permit the writing to be about something — as opposed to everything — in the project. Inductively constructing a typology permits you, I believe, to deal effectively with both positivist-empiricist writing pressures and with postmodernist ones. Although you might be pushed by the (false) consciousness of empiricist publishers/reviewers to tell how many or what percent fit into which category, you can resist the pressure by artfully staging typology as a sociological tool that eschews counting. Max Weber, for example, did not say how many people were charismatic, legal rational, or traditional in their exercise of authority, and nor did the prolific taxonomist Talcott Parsons specify numerical frequencies for any of his categorical designations. The purpose of a typology is to offer categories — not to fill in the cells.

Some of the postmodernist problems with typologies, further, can be blunted by the way one constructs and presents them. Issues of representation, authority, and authorial presence can be attended to through considerations such as the following: presenting the typology as a sociohistorical construction rather than a universal or eternal one; grounding the categories in the lived experiences of people; inductively constructing the typology; analyzing how your implicit moral stance is conveyed through such devices as the labels attached to categories (what is labeled deviant, what is devalued, etc.), the ordering of the categories in the schema, the amount of space given to discussion of each category, and so on; and revising — "re-visioning" — by decentering your authority, and privileging those who have been marginalized in texts.

THE CONTINUUM

Another rhetorical frame for qualitative papers, particularly useful for in-progress writing, is the *continuum,* an imaginary construction of an *X* along which objects (people, events, processes, things) can be arrayed. It is a modest approach, a way of looking at *some* material in a *particular* way at this *particular* time, and can thus be positioned within the postmodernist critique. If you do not reinscribe the idea of endpoints to a continuum, a metaphor borrowed from a branch of mathematics and useful for quantitative analyses, then you can "play" with poststructuralist ideas of continuity and discreteness, and reveal the dualisms in your work. For example, gender research posited a masculine/feminine continuum with masculine being at one end of the continuum, and feminine at the other end. This continuum reinscribed sex-stereotypes and binary thinking about the nature of men and women. Gender researchers now think about masculinity and femininity as fluid, situational, historical, and so on. This open-ended approach to continuum construction helps us to think about changes and differences, a postmodernist impulse, rather than fixedness and sameness.

Early in the research on the Other Woman, I hypothesized a power-imbalance continuum, such that whoever had the greatest power—which was usually, but not always, the male—had the most to gain and the least to suffer at the termination of the relationship. By conceptualizing a power-imbalance continuum I was able to look at how power interacted with gender, rather than assuming it did so in some prescribed way (1979b). That analysis broke down my dualistic thinking about gender (male/female), decentered the idea of a universal other woman, and forced me to look for differences and distinctions between women.

GETTING FEEDBACK

Whatever the rhetorical stance, though, presenting material in a public forum early in the project helps researchers hear what they are, perhaps, nonreflexively believing about their material, because listeners respond to *tone* more than they do to content. Audience comments on early papers, such as, "Why are you so hard on men?" and "Why are you so hard on single women?" and "Why are you opposed to marriage?" had me thinking that my findings were a projective test and that people were projecting on to the study their own moral (or personal) circumstances. Although some listeners/readers will always be "tone deaf," and although there will always be multiple interpretations of a text, what the author learns from the mishearing/misreading is how the writing tone may be off, tentative, or inexplicitly shifting keys—or how your authorial intentions are unfocused, ambivalent, or undermined by striking false literary notes. The multiple responses push you into examining your hidden agendas and uncertainties. You cannot finally control how readers will respond to your work, but you can use literary devices to up the odds in favor of others understanding your point of view—that is of responding to what you *intend* to communicate. Since authorial intentions reflect the moral and political position of the writer, these matters are not simply literary.

Later Papers

As the researcher's understanding of the researched world deepens and expands, how one can shape the material also deepens and expands. The writing options are many. In a complex project there are multiple events, parts, and processes and multiple insights and theoretical possibilities. Others, such as Denzin (1989), Fox (1985), Glaser and Strauss (1967), Long (1988), and Van Maanen (1988), and Wolcott (1990) provide some excellent general guidance for writing qualitative articles, and the preceding section of this book is also relevant to that problem. You may decide, for example, that a more complete typology or more complex continua are good devices for displaying your findings. Or you may want to write a more experimental, reflexive, or "confessional" piece (see Van Maanen, 1988). The stylistic opportunities for social science writers in the postmodernist context in which we live are many and enticing.

In this section I want to focus on the problem of shaping qualitative research into papers for positivist-empiricist social science journals, for example, *The American Sociological Review, Social Forces,* and *The American Journal of Sociology.* Many qualitative researchers believe that it is nearly impossible to get a paper accepted in these journals and therefore do not submit papers to them. Yet, academics are hired, tenured, and promoted on the basis of their publications in these journals; these are the journals that define disciplinary boundaries and socialize graduate students. Qualitative researchers may lament the domination of positivist-empiricist journals, but they need to acknowledge—if only to undermine—the power of these journals to "discipline" the discipline.

Shaping qualitative material for mainline journals requires telling your research story in a way that meets the expectations of the editors/reviewers of those journals. Quantitative writers have an easier time with this, for their work is already strongly encoded as positivist-empiricist (through such rhetorical devices as tables and path diagrams) and because the criteria for judging the work is more precise and shared among the community of believers. Qualitative writers have a more difficult time, I think, because their papers have fewer strong encodings, and their reviewers have fewer and less

54

precise agreements about significance and other such matters, making it difficult for the editor to say revise and resubmit and even more difficult for the writer to figure out how to revise and resubmit. Also, there is the belief that the articles should be published before the book, which makes considerable sense for findings from quantitative work (which rarely become a book, anyway), but less sense for qualitative research, because it is usually not until you have finished writing a book that you have digested, expanded, and *theorized* your work sufficiently to be able to compress it or reframe it for submission to a major social science journal.

In the case of the single woman/married man project, I decided, *after* the trade book had already been published, that I wanted to shape some of the material into an article for publication in *The American Sociological Review.* I wanted (my) graduate students to feel more confidence in the publishability of qualitative work in mainline journals, and I wanted the study's content to enter sociology's consciousness. I also wanted to redeem myself, professionally, feeling that the unexpected media attention to my trade book had besmirched my reputation. But mostly I wanted the writing challenge: Could I turn a piece of work that had four strikes against it — methodology, topic, perspective, media attention — into an *ASR* article without compromising myself as a politically situated actor?

In shaping the article, I chose the emotional, sociological, and political center of the book: how social arrangements, particularly secrecy, facilitated single women falling in love with married men and, how these liaisons favored men, as a class, over women, as a class. The editor's and reviewers' comments on early drafts were very helpful. I treated their comments as genuine questions generated by their empiricist discourse and/or indicators of textual faults (tone, clarity, point-of-view, narrative stance, etc.), rather than as attacks upon the value of the work. I thought of the reviewers not as rigid empiricist enemies but as audience, and I integrated their readings of my text into its reshaping. Their comments invited me into their discourse. Based on my writing/reading of my own text and my reading of the reviewers' readings of my writings, I re-visioned and wrote a paper that did finally appear in the *American Sociological Review* (1988b).

NARRATIVE STANCE

After several false starts, bouts of self-doubt, and lots of thinking time, I finally wrote the paper from the narrative stance of what I have come to think of as the *limited sociologist.* I explicitly positioned myself within the taken-for-granted apparatus of normal social science, which requires identifying oneself with a theoretical tradition and methodological approach. Labeling the paper is a writing convention that helps the reader know how to read the paper. I identified myself with social constructionist symbolic interactionism and, then, in a normal social science move, callously challenged that tradition for overlooking an important conceptual linkage, the linkage between status and secrecy. I did not write cynically but saw the sociological audience as a genuine audience to whom I wanted to speak.

My rhetorical plan was to make *limited* claims for the statistical *representativeness* of my findings—but *unlimited* claims to their *generality* and *theoretical significance*. This plan guided my writing decisions and demanded textual staging beginning with the title and the first two paragraphs of the paper.

The title of the paper, "Secrecy and Status: The Social Construction of Forbidden Relationships" (Richardson, 1988b), keyed two core sociological concepts, status and relationship, identified a theoretical home, social construction; and signaled new conceptual links, secrecy *and* status and *forbidden* relationships. The specific substantive content (single women/married men) was absent, as were feminist and trade encodings. The paper begins:

> Eighty years ago, Georg Simmel proposed that all social relationships "can be characterized by the amount and kind of secrecy within them and around them" (1950, p. 331). Yet, how status and secrecy affect the construction of a social relationships has been little studied. The purpose of this paper is to theorize how status and secrecy affect the construction of a particular category of relationships: secret, forbidden, sexual relationships. (p. 209)

Tradition ("Eighty years ago"), authority ("Georg Simmel"), sociology ("social relationships"), importance ("all;" "yet, . . ."), implicit measurability ("amount and kind"), conceptual linkage ("secrecy and status"), theoretical level ("purpose . . . is to theorize"), theoretical tradition ("construction"), specific citation ([1950, p. 331]), research focus ("particular category"), and categorizability ("category of relationships") all are deployed in the first paragraph. There is no "I" here, no identified author; rather, I speak as a disembodied authority in the omniscient voice of science. For good measure, the second sentence is written in the passive voice, eliminating human agency in others' research endeavors, as well. The tone is matter-of-fact, and the language is plain, the metaphors being those that go unnoticed by sociologists (e.g., status, relationship, and the grammatical demarcation of subject and object.) These are all rhetorical devices to signal the paper as mainline sociology.

The first paragraph, however, ends on a potentially suspect note: "secret, forbidden, sexual relationships." Can these be of "general" sociological interest, an *ASR* criterion, given sociology's penchant for public, legitimated, and asexual relationships? Because "secret, forbidden, sexual relationships," moreover, are grammatically set off in the text by a semicolon and positioned as the last three words of the paragraph, I have given them a very strong placement. They cannot be ignored. Was this a wise rhetorical move on my part? *ASR* conventions require that you tell the reader what your problem is in the first paragraph, so telling something is unavoidable. My decision was to cloak the specific something (the data base of single women/married men), but to *accentuate* "secret, forbidden, sexual relationships," and then make the case that these were not trivial, uncommon, rare, or without theoretical significance. The eventual acceptance of the paper, I felt, depended upon my convincing the reviewers, first, that the *category* of relationships fulfilled the generality criterion, and second that the *particular* case (single women/married men) was theoretically and empirically *paradigmatic* of the category.

WRITING "GENERALITY"

The task of the second paragraph, then, was to convince readers that there was something of *general* sociological interest going on in the paper they were about to read, not just sex or deviance, and to prepare them through the *subtext* for the substantive focus. Because the readers probably hold a number of cultural stereotypes about the topic, it was especially important to write a sociologically forceful second paragraph. To do this, I returned immediately to Simmel, tradition, citations, and sociological concepts, writing:

> The secret, to paraphrase Simmel (1950, p. 330), was one of the major achievements of humankind because it permitted an immense enlargement of the world, the possibility of hiding reality and creating a second world alongside the manifest one. The secret, he argued, is a general sociological form of major significance, regardless of its content. Because some measure of secrecy exists in all relationships, ignoring it limits our understanding of how social relationships are constructed and maintained. (1988b, p. 209)

Secrets, in this paragraph, are elevated to "major achievements," "a general form," and of "major significance" *"regardless of content."* Secrecy exists in "all relationships," and, therefore, unless we understand it (wherever it exists), our understanding of "how [all] social relationships" are constructed is "limited." While secrets are made rhetorically central to sociological understanding, the subtext of illicit relationships as *sociological worlds* — a second world alongside the manifest one, as interesting (maybe more so) and as valid a world to study (regardless of content) — is introduced and *legitimated* through reliance upon Simmel's authority in these matters. The exact focus of the project has not yet been stated but the argument for its importance has been framed. (It is an argument, incidentally, that I not only staged but believe.)

From here on through the end of the introduction, the task is to maintain the narrative stance and advance the case for the generality and importance of the research. Writing the introduction *deductively* is one of the most important literary devices. The actual *inductive* processes that characterize qualitative research in general, and my research in particular, are masked. The social science model of writing, in effect, requires researchers to suppress the story of their own research, the human processes through which their work was constituted over time. Deductively staged writing seems godlike, objective, eternal, and true — rather than human, positioned, temporal, and partially true, which it is, as all writing is — and therefore consonant with the preferred science writing model. It is not until the final paragraph of the Introduction that "I" appear, but even then, not as an observer but as a theory generator.

Throughout the introduction, I hold the (mono)tone of disinterest, develop the conceptual argument, cite appropriate authorities, and provide evidence for the endemic prevalence of "secret, forbidden, sexual" liaisons, with the single woman/married man relationship finally singled out as the paradigmatic exemplar. Drawing upon a diverse literature in gender, marriage and the family, culture studies, and demography positions the article within multiple sociological discourses, engaging readers who read through different encodings. The gender literature plays a special role in the paper, because it signals to feminists the paper's relevance to feminist agendas.

WRITING METHODS AND "FINDINGS"

The procedures section, which is requisite and positioned second in the article, is relatively long, detailing the standard methods issues regarding in-depth interviewing, sampling, reliability, validity, and representativeness, but it is a section in which "I," the researcher, exist. Readers of the *ASR* want to know about methods because procedures rank high within the logico-empiricist metaphors and models of rationality. For qualitative researchers, who usually work inductively, writing out specific procedures may feel both troublesome and falsifying. I saw my task, though, as finding ways to write within the logico-empiricist discursive space — to talk to this audience as respectfully as I would to the people I was studying. By taking the writerly (and psychological) position that empiricists were curious about the methods, not sitting back ready to demolish my procedures, I could write straightforwardly and nondefensively about the methods, issues, and processes that are of concern to them. Rhetorically, I again highlighted generality, concluding the section:

> All generalizations are based on the dominant pattern or the clear majority of respondents. When I quote from a particular interview, it represents a common interview theme. Since the interviews were open and fluid, not all respondents volunteered all themes. However, I do not discuss themes or processes that are not general. (1988b, p. 212)

Placing generality claims at the conclusion of the procedures section privileges it and prepares the reader for the substantive material to follow.

Rather than writing the results in a single section called findings, I shaped the material into two sections paralleling the two stages ("Stage One: Becoming Confidants" and "Stage Two: Becoming a We") in the process of intimacy construction. The rhetorical devices of stages and gerunds ("Becoming") prepare the reader (and prime the writer) for a *narrative,* the linking of sequential events in a storylike, causal way. However, because the story is being told in the *ASR*, the plot line is frequently interrupted by sociological analysis and commentary by the reemerged omniscient scientist. "I" am gone. The writing problem is simultaneously to tell the Other Woman's collective story, which is the finding, and explicitly moor it in sociological discourse, thereby displaying its face validity, generality, and sociological credibility.

Several literary techniques were deployed to accomplish this writing task. First, the Stage sections begin with theoretical statements, citations, and announcement of findings and the order in which I will discuss them. That is, I give the plot away; I do not write a mystery story, as I did for *The New Other Woman.* Throughout these findings sections, I weave back and forth from theoretical questions and other people's research findings to the concrete experiences and voices of the women I interviewed, tying the voices to the theory, the theory to the voices. I never stay very long at either level, because I want the collective story to be tied, in the reader's mind, with its sociological significance. As a result, I integrate quotations within paragraphs, avoiding entirely the qualitative writing conventions of long quotes, many quotes, and indented quotes, because these tend to call attention to themselves rather than to the text in which they are framed.

Similarly, I use other literary devices — such as sentence structure, phrase length, images and metaphors, jargon, paragraphing — to sustain the rhetorical thrust of the article and to suppress some narrative elements. None of the quoted women, for example, have a name or biographical history; the social production of the interviews, an interactive event that I staged, is absent; and the women's voices are written as examples, deploying what ethnomethodologists might call the taken-for-granted assumption that something can be simultaneously unique and general.

The concluding section, discussion, begins with a review of theoretically relevant findings, latches onto an analysis of marriage privilege, and concludes with a feminist/progressive message. I textually prepare for the concluding message through the ordering of the findings. The last two elements listed are "how the man's marital status is structurally conducive to idealization of the relationship; and how prioritizing the man's marital status disempowers the women" (1988b, p. 217). These are linked to the discussions of "status," "marital status," "man's marital status," and "gender and power," which are "logically" demanded by the prior framing. After drawing analogies with other secret power-imbalanced relationships, I conclude:

Secret relationships protect the interests of those with the greater status and power . . . Status differences are carried into the forbidden liaison, and rules are generated that protect the person with the higher status. In a very profound sense, then, secret, forbidden, sexual relationships are no sociological surprise. They reinforce and perpetuate the interests of the powerful. (p. 218)

The textual staging prepares the reader for the standpoint of the last paragraph, when at last I can shed the posture of the limited sociologist and recover — or uncover — my own voice as an activist sociologist, who has values and politics that will be heard even in this science journal. Synecdoche, once again, has been an (hidden) ally.

9. WRITING FOR MASS CIRCULATION

For various reasons — the topic, the energetic publicity of *The New Other Woman* by the staff of the Free Press, a book tour, and my desire to reach diverse audiences and to have some control over what they heard about it — I wrote articles for mass-circulation magazines, such as *Psychology Today* (1986a) and *Woman* (1986b). I also wrote a monthly answer column for a (now defunct) national magazine, *Q,* and worked with journalists who were writing under their own by-line.

For all of these ventures, I was contacted by the media. The media have a voracious appetite for that which is new, and they have a copy-cat norm, so that if a reference to your work appears in a high-audience channel, such as *The New York Times, Newsweek,* or "The Today Show," it is likely that many other print, television, and radio venues will be calling you. Working with the media is time consuming and energy taking. And although the current desire of many national social scientific associations is for its members to communicate their research to the mass media (in order to improve the image of social science, affect policy decisions, and replenish diminishing funding for social scientific research), the academic who does so may be subtly censored for engaging in popularization. Of all the activities I did, I liked writing the advice column best, because it gave me an opportunity to apply sociology to everyday problems of real people. It was the least demanding of concentrated effort, the least interrupting, and the activity that I felt could have a wide impact.

Writing for mass-circulation magazines, however, poses some different literary and rhetorical problems than writing a trade book or academic articles. Because there are many tricks, conventions, and norms about writing for mass circulation, I would suggest that any social scientist who is really serious about doing this (for a living, for example) take courses on magazine (and other kinds of mass market) writing in journalism departments. What I want to do in this brief section is simply to point to some of the issues and some resolutions to them for the occasional mass-market writer.

One of the major problems in writing for mass-market magazines is the very fact that the social scientific material is appearing in a mass-market magazine. Magazines employ "hyper" rhetorical devices — such as catchy titles, flashy artwork, boldface leads, and snappy side-bars — over which you have no control. Articles in these magazines tend to be hyped and presented in ways that catch the reader's attention, but may undermine your goals. One of the problems of writing for such magazines, then, is the inability to affect (never mind, control) the layout and hype surrounding your work. So, for example, although *The New Other Woman* was *not* about single women breaking up marriages, mass-circulation *articles* displayed such stereotypical illustrations as broken wedding bands, two women fighting it out, two women looking miserable, two women looking misty eyed at one man, and so on.

Further, national magazines have large staffs of editors and copy editors who are eager to rewrite your writing to sound like all the other articles in their magazine. Typically, mass-circulation articles have components such as lead-in ministories about "Tami and Ben" and "Jennifer and Josh," quotes from experts on the topic, resolutions to ministories, and some kind of how-to component. Some feminist and progressive magazines edit by committee. All of them have fairly fierce editorial policing. Consequently, one of the major problems for the social scientists writing for mass circulation is maintaining some control over their own voice.

One method for maintaining some control over your voice in mass-circulation magazines it to make sure you are *present* in your article as the *authority* on the topic. Unlike the journalists, who interview you as the expert and write scenarios about (what they call) the expert victims, you can write a first-person narrative as the *authority*. This narrative stance gives you considerable power over your material and considerable bargaining power with the editors at the magazine.

A second problem is to write enough within the expectations of the genre to interest the reader, but enough outside the genre to avoid sounding journalistic. Most of us are not very successful at writing like journalists. Doing so, moreover, undermines the basis for our credibility — that we are social scientists. Fortunately, there are ways to write social science for mass circulation. But rather than developing a whole glossary of writing conventions and techniques here, I will touch upon a few that I think make a major difference.

Literary devices such as narrative stance, concreteness, immediacy, metaphor, and story telling are ways of communicating social science to mass audiences. The *narrative stance* in mass markets can be (should be?) that of the expert with academic credentials who did the research. The stance is frankly not very postmodern, but it works if you want to reach large audiences, and there is a kind of pleasure in writing yourself into the text. Unlike the omniscient narrator in the trade book, my narrative stance in mass-circulation articles is that of a researcher. I am an "I" who interviewed women, and I appear throughout the text. Such phrases as "told to me," "I find," "I believe," and "I interviewed" ground the text in my activity as a bona fide researcher.

Concrete examples, however, are the primary literary device used in writing for mass markets. When a general point is being made, statistics, examples, and quotations enter the text to illustrate and document the point. Preferable are examples that resonate with the particular *audience.* In the *Psychology Today* article (1986a), for example, after saying that in a liaison with a married man, "the Other Woman gradually loses control of how her time is spent," I document that statement with the experience of a bank vice president, a divorced woman who managed a staff of 50, who described in detail "the fatal flaw in the relationship." She said,

> The flaw was that he really was in charge, even when I thought I was. When it finally came down to it, he thought I should stop what I was doing when he came over, even when he knew I had deadlines to meet. He really did not respect the importance of my work to me. (p. 27)

I follow the banker's lament with the story of a dentist who did not schedule noontime appointments because sometimes her lover "shook time loose" at midday. The women are socioeconomically similar to the readers; the time management issues resonate. These concrete examples, further, carry a larger message of the article, that the "advantages [of a liaison] are often out-weighed by high costs" (p. 27).

Immediacy, another important literary device, is accomplished in several ways. Consider the following excerpt from the *Psychology Today* article:

> Being the Other Woman appears to be a workable solution for many contemporary single women. Some in my study are quite successful in limiting their emotional involvement. They come through their liaisons feeling empowered . . . But then there are those who are hurt and disappointed . . . They lose control over their feelings, become totally invested in the affair, and end up deriving more pain than pleasure. (p. 27)

"Being," a gerund implying "now" and "whole," begins the paragraph, immediately followed by "the Other Woman," a "new" conceptualization as implied by its capitalization, and concluded with "contemporary," an explicit reference to "now." In the second sentence, "I" ("my study") appear as an active writer-researcher in conversation with the reader. Throughout the paragraph the verb tense is in the present, the sentences are relatively short, as are the words. Action is written as happening now ("lose control" . . . "become invested" . . . "end up"). All of these devices contribute to a sense of immediacy.

As has been discussed earlier in this book, *metaphor and imagery* play a major role in communicating content. This is true for mass-market writing, as well. When the content is nonnormative, it is especially important that the metaphors work for you. One "Other Woman" article is structured through the large metaphor of "another world," which resonates with the soap opera, as well as the Harlequin Romance, and, as the mass reader learns, with Georg Simmel's ideas about secrecy, as well. On a simpler level, I look for images that fit the tone of the article and do not wave unnecessary red flags. For example, I talk about cultural bulwark rather than ideology, and male privilege rather than patriarchy.

But the major rhetorical device I use, which should be no surprise to you the reader, is constructing the article as a sociological *narrative* that encircles the many individual, yet general, narratives of the women who told me about their lives.

CONCLUSION

How we write lives is important, theoretically and practically. Civic discourse about societal identity, social goals, and societal transformation is largely constituted through social scientific language (Brown, 1977). The rhetorics of the social sciences identify and shape our social past, present, and future. They are well-nigh unavoidable in modern societies. At issue, then, is not the presence of social scientific narratives and rhetorics but *what* kind(s) of social-scientific representation do we foster, and with what consequences for whom.

Writing as we are within a larger contemporary context that undermines claims to authority, universality, and eternal truth, we are newly challenged. We can freeze into political inaction and atrophied moral consciousness. Or we can interpret the current intellectual climate as giving us the opportunity to write reflexively. We can understand our work as sites of moral and political activity. It is the latter choice that I have made, and that I have argued for in this book.

If there is no final authority or final solution to issues of truth, one can only look for partial, temporal, historical resolutions. Such looking brings us to moral questions, about which there are more or less principled resolutions. I submit that a more principled solution is one that has as its intention the textual enfranchisement of the previously disenfranchised. Writing is, thus, not opposed to practice but *is* a political practice (Lather, 1988). The theory versus praxis opposition is dismantled, relieving academics, should they so choose, of feigned innocence, on the hand, and bewailed impotence, on the other.

As privileged writers with skills and access to publics, as I have argued earlier, we can use our positions to advance the case of the nonprivileged. The task is to tell their stories in such a way that the writing "resists its own subordination to a putatively more significant practice of production," to rules of writing that thoughtlessly reproduce subordination and a "generically unalterable" enveloping society (Agger, 1989a). One way of doing this rewriting — of interrupting the reproduction of sociological knowledge as the "cartographer of domination" (Agger, 1989a) and postmodernist discourse as the cosmographer of ennui — is to reveal narrative as the centerpiece of the human sciences.

People make sense of their lives, for the most part, in terms of specific events, such as giving birth, and sequences of events, such as the life-long impact of parenting a damaged child. Most people do not articulate how the sociological categories of race, gender, class, and ethnicity have shaped their lives or how the larger historical processes such as the demographic transition, service economies, and the Women's Movement have affected them. Erik Erikson (1975) contends that only great people, people who see themselves as actors upon an historical stage, tell their life stories in a larger and historical context. Yet, as C. Wright Mills cogently argued (1959, p. 5), knowledge of the social context leads people to understand their own experiences and to gauge their own fates. This is the promise of the sociological imagination. What social scientists are capable of is giving voice to silenced people, presenting them as historical actors by telling their collective stories.

Rhetorically, through curricula, grants, honorees, and written exemplars of core social science in core social science journals, the belief that narrative is (at best) of marginal interest — and certainly a nonproblematic for practicing sociologists — is reproduced and reconstituted term after term in academia. Yet, as the new rhetoric of the social sciences has made clear, rhetorical decisions are constantly being made, often unconsciously, by the practitioners (see Nelson, Megill, and McCloskey, 1987). We choose how we write. Those choices have poetic, rhetorical, ethical, and political implications.

Marginalizing of the narrative may serve the political interests of entrenched social scientific elites, but it does not serve the social sciences or society. Narratives exist at the everyday, autobiographical, biographical, cultural, and collective levels. They reflect the universal human experience of time and link the past, present, and future. Narrative links sociology to literature and to history. The human experience of stability and transformation becomes sociologically accessible. Narrative gives room for the expression of our individual and shared fates, our personal and communal worlds. Narrative permits the individual, the society, or the group to explain its experiences of temporality, because narrative attends to and grows out of temporality. It is the universal way in which humans accommodate to finitude. Narrative is the best way to understand the human experience, because it is the way humans understand their own lives. It is the closest to the human experience and hence the least falsifying of that experience, and it rejuvenates the sociological imagination in the service of liberatory civic discourses and transformative social projects.

Finally, narrative suggests an answer to the questions that have driven this book: How and for whom should we write? If we wish to understand the deepest and most universal of human experiences, if we wish our work to be faithful to the lived experiences of people, if we wish for a union between poetics and science, if we wish to reach a variety of readers, or if we wish to use our privileges and skills to empower the people we study, then we need to *foreground,* not suppress, the narrative within the human sciences. How and for whom we write lives matters.

REFERENCES

Agger, Ben (1989a) Socio(onto)logy: A Disciplinary Reading. Urbana: University of llinois.

Agger, Ben (1989b) "Do books write authors?: A study of disciplinary hegemony." Teaching Sociology 17: 365-369.

Agger, Ben (1990) The Decline of Discourse: Reading, Writing and Resistance in Postmodern Capitalism. Bristol, PA: Falmer.

Barthes, Roland (1966) Introduction to the Structural Analysis of the Narrative. Occasional Paper, Centre for Contemporary Cultural Studies, University of Birmingham.

Bazerman, Charles (1988) Shaping Written Knowledge: The Genre and Activity of the Experimental Article in Science. Madison: University of Wisconsin Press.

Becker, Howard S. (1986a) Writing for Social Scientists: How to Finish Your Thesis, Book, or Article. Chicago: The University of Chicago Press.

Bertaux-Wiame, Isabelle (1981) "The life history approach to the study of internal migration," pp. 249-265 in Daniel Bertaux (ed.) Biography and Society: The Life History Approach in the Social Sciences. Beverly Hills, CA: Sage.

Brown, Richard H. (1977) A Poetic for Sociology. Cambridge: Cambridge University Press.

Bruner, Edward M. (1986) "Ethnography as narrative," pp. 137-55 in Victor Turner and Edward M. Bruner (eds.) The Anthropology of Experience. Urbana: University of Illinois Press.

Bruner, Jerome (1986) Actual Minds, Possible Worlds. Cambridge, MA: Harvard University Press.

Buker, Eloise (in press) "Hidden desires and missing persons: A feminist deconstruction of Foucault." Western Political Quarterly.

Campbell, John Angus (1987) "Charles Darwin: Rhetorician of science," pp. 69-86 in John S. Nelson, Allan Megill, and Donald N. McCloskey (eds). The Rhetoric of the Human Sciences: Language and Argument in Scholarship and Public Affairs. Madison: University of Wisconsin Press.

Cheal, David (1989) Family Theory after the Big Bang: Postmodern Knowledge and the Sociology of the Family. Paper presented at the American Sociological Association Annual Meetings, San Francisco, CA.

Clifford, James (1986) "Introduction: Partial truths," pp. 1-26 in James Clifford and George E. Marcus (eds.) Writing Culture: The Poetics and Politics of Ethnography. Berkeley: University of California Press.

Clifford, James and George E. Marcus (eds.) (1986) Writing Culture: The Poetics and Politics of Ethnography. Berkeley: University of California Press.

Clough, Patricia (1987) "Feminist theory and social psychology." Studies in Symbolic Interaction 8: 3-22.

De Certau, Michael (1983) "History: Ethics, science and fiction," pp. 173-209 in Norma Hahn, Robert Bellah, Paul Rabinaw, and William Sullivan (eds.) Social Science as Moral Inquiry. New York: Columbia University Press.

Deegan, Mary Jo (1988) Jane Addams and the Men of the Chicago School, 1892-1918. New Brunswick, NJ: Transaction Books.

Denzin, Norman K. (1986) "A postmodern social theory." Sociological Theory 4: 194-204.

Denzin, Norman K. (1987) The Alcoholic Self. Newbury Park, CA: Sage.

Denzin, Norman K. (1989) Interpretive Biography. Newbury Park, CA: Sage.

Derrida, Jacques (1982) Margins of Philosophy (Alan Bass, Trans.). Chicago: University of Chicago Press.

Eagleton, Terry (1983) Literary Theory: An Introduction. Minneapolis: University of Minnesota Press.

Edmondson, Ricca (1984) Rhetoric in Sociology. London: Macmillan.

Ellis, Carolyn (1989, August) "What are You Feeling?": Issues in the Introspective Method. Paper presented at the American Sociological Association Annual Meetings, San Francisco, CA.

Erikson, Erik H. (1980) Identity and the Life Cycle. New York: Norton.

Erikson, Kai T. (1976) Everything in Its Path: Destruction of the Community in the Buffalo Creek Flood. New York: Simon & Schuster.

Ferraro, Kathleen J. and John M. Johnson (1983) "How women experience battering: The process of victimization." Social Problems 30(3): 325-339.

Fisher, Walter R. (1987) Human Communication as Narration: Toward a Philosophy of Reason, Value, and Action. Columbia: University of South Carolina Press.

Flax, Jane (1987) "Postmodernism and gender relations in feminist theory." Signs 12: 621-643.

Fox, Mary Frank (ed.) (1985) Scholarly Writing and Publishing: Issues, Problems and Solutions. Boulder, CO: Westview.

Fraser, Nancy and Linda Nicholson (1988) "Social criticism without philosophy: An encounter between feminism and postmodernism," pp. 83-104 in Andrew Ross (ed.) Universal Abandon: The Politics of Postmodernism. Minneapolis: University of Minnesota Press.

Frye, Northrop (1957) Anatomy of Criticism. Princeton: Princeton University Press.

Glaser, Barney G. and Anselm L. Strauss (1967) The Discovery of Grounded Theory: Strategies for Qualitative Research. Chicago: Aldine.

Gleick, James (1984, June 10) "Solving the mathematical riddle of chaos." The New York Times Magazine, pp. 30-32.

Gusfield, Joseph (1976) "The literary rhetoric of science: Comedy and pathos in drinking driver research." American Sociological Review 4: 16-34.

Haraway, Donna (1988) "Situated knowledges: The science question in feminism and the privilege of partial perspective." Feminist Studies 14: 575-599.

Harding, Sandra (1986) The Science Question in Feminism. Ithaca, NY: Cornell University Press.

Hassan, Ihab (1987) The Postmodern Turn: Essays in Postmodern Theory and Culture. Columbus: Ohio State University Press.

Heisenberg, Werner (1965) "Non-objective science and uncertainty," pp. 444-452 in Richard Ellman and Charles Feidelson, Jr. (eds.) The Modern Tradition: Backgrounds of Modern Literature. New York: Oxford University Press.

Husserl, Edmond (1964) The Phenomenology of Internal Time Consciousness (James S. Churchill, Trans.). Bloomington: Indiana University Press.

Hutcheon, Linda (1988) A Poetics of Postmodernism: History, Theory, Fiction. New York: Routledge.

Jakobson, Roman (1960) "Linguistics and poetry," pp. 350-377 in Thomas A. Sebock (ed.) Style and Language. Cambridge, MA: MIT Press.

Jameson, Fredric (1981) The Political Unconscious. Ithaca, NY: Cornell University Press.

Kanter, Rosabeth (1980) Men and Women of the Corporation. Homewood, IL: Dorsey Press.

Kaufman, Sharon R. (1986) The Ageless Self: Sources of Meaning in Later Life. Madison: University of Wisconsin Press.

Kline, Morris (1980) Mathematics: The Loss of Certainty. New York: Oxford University Press.

Kohli, Martin (1981) "Biography: Account, text, method," pp. 61-75 in Daniel Bertaux (ed.) Biography and Society: The Life History Approach in the Social Sciences. Beverly Hills, CA: Sage.

Krieger, Susan (1983) The Mirror Dance: Identity in a Woman's Community. Philadelphia: Temple University Press.

Lakoff, George and Mark Johnson (1980) Metaphors We Live By. Chicago: University of Chicago Press.

Lather, Patti (1986) "Research as praxis." Harvard Educational Review 56: 257-277.

Lather, Patti (1988) Postmodernism and the Politics of Enlightenment. Paper presented at the National Women's Studies Association Annual Meetings, Minneapolis, MN.

Lather, Patti (1989, October) Deconstructing/Deconstructive Inquiry: The Politics of Knowing and Being Known. Paper presented at the American Educational Research Association Conference, San Francisco, CA.

Levine, Donald N. (1985) The Flight from Ambiguity: Essays in Social and Cultural Theory. Chicago: University of Chicago Press.

Lewis, Oscar (1970) The Children of Sanchez: An Autobiography of a Mexican Family. New York: Random House.

Liebow, Elliot (1967) Tally's Corner: A Study of Negro Streetcorner Men. Washington, DC: Catholic University Press.

Linden, R. Ruth (1989) Making Stories, Making Selves: The Holocaust, Identity and Memory. Unpublished doctoral dissertation, Department of Sociology, Brandeis University.

Long, Judy (1988, August) Rhetorics of Gender in Social Science. Paper presented at the Annual American Sociological Association Meeting, Atlanta.

Lyotard, Jean-Francois (1979) The Postmodern Condition: A Report on Knowledge. (Geoff Bennington and Brian Massumi, Trans.). Minneapolis: University of Minnesota Press.

Maines, David (1989, March) The Storied Nature of Diabetic Self-Help Groups. Paper presented at the Gregory Stone Symbolic Interaction Symposium, Arizona State University, Tempe, AZ.

Manning, Peter (1989, August) Strands in the Postmodernist Rope: Oxymorons in the Desert. Paper presented at the Society for the Study of Symbolic Interactionism Meetings, San Francisco.

Marcus, George E. and Michael M. J. Fisher (1986) Anthropology as Cultural Critique: An Experimental Moment in the Human Sciences. Chicago: University of Chicago Press.

McClelland, David C. (1961) The Achieving Society. New York: Free Press.

McCloskey, Donald N. (1985) The Rhetoric of Economics. Madison: University of Wisconsin Press.

Mills, C. Wright (1959) The Sociological Imagination. New York: Oxford University Press.

Morris, Meaghan (1988) The Pirate's Fiancee: Feminism, Reading, and Postmodernism. London and New York: Verso.

Nelson, John S., Alan Megill, and Donald N. McCloskey (eds.) (1987) The Rhetoric of the Human Sciences: Language and Argument in Scholarship and Human Affairs. Madison: University of Wisconsin Press.

Nicholson, Linda J. (ed.) (1990) Feminism and Postmodernism. New York: Routledge.

Polkinghorne, Donald E. (1988) Narrative Knowing and The Human Sciences. Albany: State University of New York Press.

Powell, Walter W. (1985) Getting into Print: The Decision-Making Process in Scholarly Publishing. Chicago: University of Chicago Press.

Reinharz, Shulamit (1979) On Becoming a Social Scientist. San Francisco: Jossey-Bass.

Richardson, Laurel [Walum] (1979a) "The end of the long affair: The perspective of the 'Other Woman.' " Alternative Lifestyles 2(4): 397-414.

Richardson, Laurel [Walum] (1979b, August) The Other Woman: "His" and "Her" Perspectives. Paper presented at the American Sociological Association Meetings, Boston, MA.

Richardson, Laurel (1985) The New Other Woman: Contemporary Single Women in Affairs with Married Men. New York: Free Press.

Richardson, Laurel (1986a) "Another world." Psychology Today 20(2): 22-27.

Richardson, Laurel (1986b) "The new other woman: Contemporary single women in affairs with married men." Woman 7(1): 44-45.

Richardson, Laurel (1987) "Disseminating research to popular audiences: The book tour." Qualitative Sociology 19(2): 164-176.

Richardson, Laurel (1988a) "The collective story: Postmodernism and the writing of sociology." Sociological Focus 21: 199-208.

Richardson, Laurel (1988b) "Secrecy and status: The social construction of forbidden relationships." American Sociological Review 53(2): 209-220.

Richardson, Laurel (1990) "Narrative and sociology." Journal of Contemporary Ethnography 9(1): 116-136.

Richardson, Laurel (in press-a) "Speakers whose voices matter." Studies in Symbolic Interactionism.

Richardson, Laurel (in press-b) "Value constituting practices, rhetoric and metaphor in sociology: A reflexive analysis." Current Perspectives in Social Theory.

Ricoeur, Paul (1984-1986) Time and Narrative. (Kathleen McLaughlin and David Pellauer, Trans.). Chicago: University of Chicago Press.

Riley, Matilda White (1988) Sociological Lives. Newbury Park, CA: Sage.

Rogers, Mary F. (1989, August) Narrative Performances and their Frames: Garfinkel, Giddens, and Goffman. Paper presented at the Annual American Sociological Association Meeting, San Francisco, CA.

Rorty, Richard (1979) Philosophy and the Mirror of Nature. Princeton: Princeton University Press.

Roth, Paul (1989) How Narratives Explain. Paper presented at the University of Iowa Faculty Rhetoric Seminar (POROI), Iowa City.

Rubin, Lillian B. (1976) Worlds of Pain: Life in the Working-Class Family. New York: Basic Books.

Schutz, Alfred (1962) Collected Papers. The Hague: Nijhoff.

Shapiro, Michael (1985-1986, Winter) "Metaphor in the philosophy of the social sciences." Cultural Critique 2: 191-214.

Shatzkin, Leonard (1982) In Cold Type: Overcoming the Book Crisis. Boston: Houghton Mifflin.

Simmel, Georg (1902-1903, 1908, 1917, 1950) The Sociology of Georg Simmel (Kurt H. Wolfe, Trans.). New York: Free Press.

Stack, Carol B. (1974) All Our Kin: Strategies for Survival in a Black Community. New York: Harper & Row.

Stewart, John O. (1989) Drinkers, Drummers and Decent Folk: Ethnographic Narratives of Village Trinidad. Albany: State University of New York Press.

Van Maanen, John (1988) Tales of the Field. Chicago: University of Chicago Press.

Whyte, William Foote (1943) Street Corner Society: The Social Structure of an Italian Slum. Chicago: University of Chicago Press.

Wolcott, Harry F. (1990) Writing Up Qualitative Research. Sage University Paper Series on Qualitative Research Methods, Vol. 20. Newbury Park, CA: Sage.

Young, T. R. (1989) Postmodern Sociology. Paper presented at the Midwest Sociological Society, Chicago. (Unpublished Manuscripts 138a and 138b, Red Feather Institute)

ABOUT THE AUTHOR

LAUREL RICHARDSON is Professor of Sociology at Ohio State University, Columbus. She is the author of several books, including *The Dynamics of Sex and Gender* (3rd ed., 1988), *Feminists Frontiers II* [with Verta Taylor] (1989), and *Gender and University Teaching* [with Anne Statham and Judith A. Cook] (in press). Her trade book, *The New Other Woman: Contemporary Single Women in Affairs with Married Men* (1985), was widely acclaimed in both professional and lay reviews and has been published in Portuguese (1988), Japanese (1988), and German (1987) editions. She has written over 40 academic articles as well as numbers of articles for mass-circulation magazines. Currently, she teaches advanced qualitative research methods, contemporary theory, and gender. She is former president of the North Central Sociological Association and serves on the American Sociological Association's Committee on Public Information.